smoke

&

blue
in
the
face

two films by

paul
auster

Library of Congress Cataloging-In-Publication Data

Auster, Paul, 1947–
    Smoke & blue in the face : two films / by Paul Auster ; with a preface by Wayne Wang.
        p.   cm.
    ISBN 0-7868-8098-8
    1. Brooklyn (New York, N.Y.)—Drama.   2. Men—New York (N.Y.)—Drama.   3. Motion picture plays.   I. Title.
    PS3551.U77S66   1995
    791.43'72—dc20   95-3652
                                                                                                            CIP

FIRST EDITION
10 9 8 7 6 5 4 3 2 1

smoke & blue in the face:
two films

with a

preface

by

wayne
wang

MIRAMAX
B O O K S

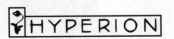
HYPERION

new york

contents

preface
by wayne wang

CHRISTMAS DAY, 1990. SAN FRANCISCO

My delivery of *The New York Times* did not come. I had to go to the neighborhood grocery store to buy one. I bought the last copy on the rack.

The paper was very thin that day. I read through it rather quickly. Except for a couple articles about the impending Gulf War, there was not much in the news. Then something caught my eye. There was a full-page article in the Op-Ed section. It was titled "Auggie Wren's Christmas Story," by Paul Auster.

As I started to read the story, I was quickly drawn into a complex world of reality and fiction, truth and lies, giving and taking. I was alternately moved to tears and laughing uncontrollably. Many of my own interesting Christmas-day experiences flashed through my mind. By the end, I felt that I had been given a wonderful Christmas gift by someone I was very close to. As soon as I finished the story, I asked my wife, "Who is Paul Auster?"

MAY 1991. BROOKLYN

I met Paul Auster for the first time at his studio in Park Slope. By now I had read most of his books. I was very excited to meet him and talk about my ideas for turning "Auggie Wren's Christmas Story" into a feature film.

Paul was very friendly, and generous with his time. We talked for a while in his studio. We had lunch at Jack's Deli (where Auggie told Paul the Christmas Story). We bought Schimmelpennincks at the cigar store that inspired the story. We walked all over Brooklyn, and Paul told me a dozen great stories about the city.

By the end of the day, as I was saying good-bye, I realized I had met a true artist who was passionate about people, life, and history. And he was committed to writing about them in his studio every day in a no-nonsense way.

That day I became more committed than ever to turning "Auggie Wren's Christmas Story" into a film.

DECEMBER 1994. NEW YORK CITY

It has now been about four years since I first read "Auggie Wren's Christmas Story." The film I was determined to make is finally finished. It is titled *Smoke*. It took a lot of economic, emotional, and creative twists and turns and ups and downs to get to this point.

I am very proud of *Smoke* and its companion, *Blue in the Face*. These two films are Christmas gifts to the moviegoing audience from Paul Auster and Wayne Wang.

I thank Paul Auster for the inspiration, for being my friend, my brother, and my partner throughout the last four years.

smoke

the making of smoke

ANNETTE INSDORF:* I gather that *Smoke* began with a Christmas story you wrote for *The New York Times*.

PAUL AUSTER: Yes, it all started with that little story. Mike Levitas, the editor of the Op-Ed page, called me out of the blue one morning in November of 1990. I didn't know him, but he had apparently read some of my books. In his friendly, matter-of-fact way he told me that he'd been toying with the idea of commissioning a work of fiction for the Op-Ed page on Christmas Day. What did I think? Would I be willing to write it? It was an interesting proposal, I thought—putting a piece of make-believe in a newspaper, the paper of record, no less. A rather subversive notion when you get right down to it. But the fact was that I had never written a short story, and I wasn't sure I'd be able to come up with an idea. "Give me a few days," I said. "If I think of something, I'll let you know." So a few days went by, and just when I was about to give up, I opened a tin of my beloved Schimmelpennincks—the little cigars I like to smoke—and started thinking about the man who sells them to me in Brooklyn. That led to some thoughts about the kinds of encounters you have in New York with people you see every day but don't really know. And little by little, the story began to take shape inside me. It literally came out of that tin of cigars.

AI: It's not what I would call your typical Christmas story.

PA: I hope not. Everything gets turned upside down in "Auggie Wren." What's stealing? What's giving? What's lying? What's telling the truth? All these questions are reshuffled in rather odd and unorthodox ways.

---

*Chair of the Film Division of Columbia University's School of the Arts and author of *François Truffaut*.

AI: When did Wayne Wang enter the picture?

PA: Wayne called me from San Francisco a few weeks after the story was published.

AI: Did you know him?

PA: No. But I knew of him and had seen one of his films, *Dim Sum,* which I had greatly admired. It turned out that he'd read the story in the *Times* and felt it would make a good premise for a movie. I was flattered by his interest, but at that point I didn't want to write the script myself. I was hard at work on a novel [*Leviathan*] and couldn't think about anything else. But if Wayne wanted to use the story to make a movie, that was fine by me. He was a good filmmaker, and I knew that something good would come of it.

AI: How was it, then, that you wound up writing the screenplay?

PA: Wayne came to New York that spring. It was May, I think, and the first afternoon we spent together we just walked around Brooklyn. It was a beautiful day, I remember, and I showed him the different spots around town where I had imagined the story taking place. We got along very well. Wayne is a terrific person, a man of great sensitivity, generosity, and humor, and unlike most artists, he doesn't make art to gratify his ego. He has a genuine calling, which means that he never feels obligated to defend himself or beat his own drum. After that first day in Brooklyn, it became clear to both of us that we were going to become friends.

AI: Were any ideas for the film discussed that day?

PA: Rashid, the central figure of the story, was born during that preliminary talk. And also the conviction that the movie would be about Brooklyn. . . . Wayne went back to San Francisco and started working with a screenwriter friend of his on a treatment. He sent it to me in August, a story outline of ten or twelve pages. I was with my family in Vermont just then, and I remember feeling that the outline was good, but not good enough. I gave it to my wife Siri to read, and that night we lay awake in bed talking through another story, a different approach altogether. I called Wayne the next day, and he agreed that this new story was better than the one he'd sent me. As a small favor to him, he asked me if I wouldn't mind writing up the treatment of this new story. I figured I owed him that much, and so I did it.

AI: And suddenly, so to speak, your foot was in the door.

PA: It's funny how these things work, isn't it? A few weeks later, Wayne went to Japan on other business. He met with Satoru Iseki of NDF [Nippon Film Development] about his project, and just in passing, in a casual sort of way, he mentioned the treatment I had written. Mr. Iseki was very interested. He'd like to produce our film, he said, but only if "Auster writes the script." My books are published in Japan, and it seemed that he knew who I was. But he would need an American partner, he said, someone to split the costs and oversee production. When Wayne called me from Tokyo to report what had happened, I laughed. The chances of Mr. Iseki ever finding an American partner seemed so slim, so utterly beyond the realm of possibility, that I said yes, I'll do the screenplay if there's money to make the film. And then I immediately went back to writing my novel.

AI: But they did find a partner, didn't they?

PA: Sort of. Tom Luddy, a good friend of Wayne's in San Francisco, wanted to do it at Zoetrope. When Wayne told me the news, I was stunned, absolutely caught off guard. But I couldn't back out. Morally speaking, I was committed to writing the script. I had given my word, and so once I finished *Leviathan* [at the end of '91], I started writing *Smoke*. A few months later, the deal between NDF and Zoetrope fell apart. But I was too far into it by then to want to stop. I had already written a first draft, and once you start something, it's only natural to want to see it through to the end.

AI: Had you ever written a screenplay before?

PA: Not really. When I was very young, nineteen or twenty years old, I wrote a couple of scripts for silent movies. They were very long and very detailed, seventy or eighty pages of elaborate and meticulous movements, every gesture spelled out in words. Weird, deadpan slapstick. Buster Keaton revisited. Those scripts are lost now. I wish to hell I knew where they were. I'd love to see what they looked like.

AI: Did you do any sort of special preparation? Did you read scripts? Did you start watching movies with a different eye toward construction?

PA: I looked at some scripts, just to make sure of the format. How to number the scenes, moving from interiors to exteriors, that kind of thing. But no real preparation—except a lifetime of watching movies. I've always been drawn to them, ever since I was a boy. It's the rare person in this world who isn't, I suppose. But at the same time, I also have certain problems with them. Not just with this or that particular movie, but with movies in general, the medium itself.

AI: In what way?

PA: The two-dimensionality, first of all. People think of movies as "real," but they're not. They're flat pictures projected against a wall, a simulacrum of reality, not the real thing. And then there's the question of the images. We tend to watch them passively, and in the end they wash right through us. We're captivated and intrigued and delighted for two hours, and then we walk out of the theater and can barely remember what we've seen. Novels are totally different. To read a book, you have to be actively involved in what the words are saying. You have to work, you have to use your imagination. And once your imagination has been fully awakened, you enter into the world of the book as if it were your own life. You smell things, you touch things, you have complex thoughts and insights, you find yourself in a three-dimensional world.

AI: The novelist speaks.

PA: Well, needless to say, I'm always going to come down on the side of books. But that doesn't mean movies can't be wonderful. It's another way of telling stories, that's all, and I suppose it's important to remember what each medium can and can't do . . . I'm particularly attracted to directors who emphasize telling stories over technique, who take the time to allow their characters to unfold before your eyes, to exist as full-fledged human beings.

AI: Who would you put in that category?

PA: Renoir, for one. Ozu for another. Bresson . . . Satyajit Ray . . . a whole range, finally. These directors don't bombard you with pictures, they're not in love with the image for its own sake. They tell their stories with all the care and patience of the best novelists. Wayne is that kind of director. Someone who has sympathy for the inner lives of his characters, who doesn't rush things. That was why I was happy to be working with him—to be working *for* him. A screenplay is no more than a blueprint, after all. It's not the finished product. I didn't write the script in a vacuum. I wrote it for Wayne, for a movie that he was going to direct, and I very consciously tried to write something that would be compatible with his strengths as a director.

AI: How long did it take you to write it?

PA: The first draft took about three weeks, maybe a month. Then the negotiations between NDF and Zoetrope broke down, and suddenly the whole project was left dangling. It was probably dumb of me to start without a signed contract, but I hadn't yet understood how iffy and unstable the movie business is. At that point, however,

NDF decided to go ahead and "develop" the script anyway while they searched for another American partner. That meant that I'd be given a little money to continue writing, and so I kept at it. Wayne and I discussed the first draft, I tinkered with it a little more, and then we both moved on to other things. Wayne went into preproduction for *The Joy Luck Club,* and I began writing a new novel [*Mr. Vertigo*]. But we stayed in close touch, and every once in a while over the next year and a half we'd talk on the phone or get together somewhere to discuss new ideas about the script.

I did about three more versions, and each time that entailed a week or two of work—adding elements, discarding elements, rethinking the structure. There's a big difference between the first draft and the final draft, but the changes happened slowly, by increments, and I never felt that I was changing the essence of the story. Gradually finding it is probably more like it. At some point in all this, Peter Newman came in as our American producer, but the money to make the movie still had to be found. Meanwhile, I kept working on *Mr. Vertigo,* and by the time I finished it, Wayne's movie was about to be released. And so there we were, ready to tackle *Smoke* again.

By some twist of good luck, Wayne decided to show the script to Robert Altman. Altman had very nice things to say about it, but he felt it lagged a bit in the middle and probably needed one more little something before it found its definitive shape. Robert Altman is not someone whose opinion should be discounted, and so I went back and reread the script with his comments in mind, and lo and behold, he was right. I sat down to work again, and this time everything seemed to fit. The story was rounder, fuller, more integrated. It was no longer a collection of fragments. It finally had some coherence to it.

AI: A very different process from writing a novel, then. Did you enjoy it?

PA: Yes, completely different. Writing a novel is an organic process, and most of it happens unconsciously. It's long and slow and very grueling. A screenplay is more like a jigsaw puzzle. Writing the actual words might not be very time-consuming, but putting the pieces together can drive you crazy. But yes, I did enjoy it. I found it a challenge to write dialogue, to think in dramatic terms rather than narrative terms, to do something I had never done before.

AI: And then Miramax stepped in and decided to back the film.

PA: *The Joy Luck Club* turned out to be a big success, the screenplay was finished, and Peter Newman happens to be a very droll and persuasive man. I was out of the country for a couple of weeks last fall, and when I came home, it seemed that we were in business. All the arrangements were in place.

AI: And that's when the screenwriter is supposed to disappear.

PA: So they say. But Wayne and I forgot to pay attention to the rules. It never occurred to either one of us to part company then. I was the writer, Wayne was the director, but it was *our* film, and all along we had considered ourselves equal partners in the project. I understand now what an unusual arrangement this was. Writers and directors aren't supposed to like each other, and no one had ever heard of a director treating a writer as Wayne treated me. But I was naive and stupid, and I took it for granted that I was still involved.

AI: Not all that naive, though. You'd been involved in another film once before— *The Music of Chance.*

PA: Yes, but that was completely different. Philip Haas adapted a novel of mine and turned that adaptation into a movie. A different story altogether. He and his wife wrote the script, and he directed it. He had a free hand to interpret the book as he chose, to present his particular reading of the book I had written. But my work was already finished before he started.

AI: Yes, but you also wound up playing a role in that film, didn't you? As an actor, I mean.

PA: True, true. My thirty-second cameo appearance in the final scene. Never again! If nothing else, I emerged from that experience with a new respect for what actors can do. I mean trained, professional actors. There's nothing like a little taste of the real thing to teach you humility.

AI: Back to *Smoke,* then. Were you involved in the casting, for example?

PA: To some degree, yes. And Wayne and I discussed every decision very thoroughly. We had some disappointments along the way, and also some very hard decisions to make. One actor I made a very intense plea for was Giancarlo Esposito. His role is very small. He plays Tommy, the OTB Man, and appears only peripherally in two scenes. But his character gets to speak the first lines in the movie, and I knew that if he accepted, things would get off to a flying start. It was a great moment for me when he said yes. The same with Forest Whitaker. I couldn't imagine any other actor playing Cyrus, and I can't tell you how thrilled I was when he agreed to do the part. . . . Other than that, I sat in on a lot of the auditions. What a heart-breaking spectacle that can be. So many talented people marching in with their high hopes and tough skins. It takes courage to court rejection on a daily basis, and I must say that I was moved by all this. . . .

Looking back on it now, though, I would say that the single most memorable experience connected with the casting was an open call organized by Heidi Levitt and Billy Hopkins. A bitter cold Saturday in late January, snow on the ground, howling winds, and three thousand people showed up at a high school in Manhattan to try out for bit parts in *Smoke*. Three thousand people! The line went all the way down the block. What a motley collection of humanity. The large and the small, the fat and the thin, the young and the old, the white, the black, the brown, the yellow . . . everyone from a former Miss Nigeria to an ex-middleweight boxing champion, and every last one of them wanted to be in the movies. I was astonished.

AI: Well, you wound up with an extraordinary cast. Harvey Keitel, William Hurt, Stockard Channing, Forest Whitaker, Ashley Judd . . . and Harold Perrineau in his first role. It's a great line-up.

PA: They were good people to work with, too. None of the actors made a lot of money, but they all seemed enthusiastic about being in the film. That made for a good working atmosphere all around. . . . About two months before shooting began, Wayne and I started meeting with the actors to discuss their roles and examine the nuances of the script. I wound up writing "Character Notes" for many of the parts, exhaustive lists and comments to help fill in the background of each character's life. Not just biographies and family histories, but the music they listened to, the foods they ate, the books they read—anything and everything that might help the actor get a handle on his role.

AI: Marguerite Duras used precisely that approach when she wrote her script for *Hiroshima Mon Amour,* one of my favorite films of all time. There is a sense of texture about the characters, even though we aren't told very much about their backgrounds.

PA: The more you know, the more helpful it is. It's not easy pretending to be someone else, after all. The more you have to hold on to, the richer your performance is going to be.

AI: I take it there were rehearsals for *Smoke*—something for which there isn't always time with movies.

PA: It seemed essential in this case, given that there's so much talk in the film and so little action! Rehearsals went on for several weeks in a church near Washington Square. Harvey, Bill, Harold, Stockard, Ashley . . . they all worked very hard.

AI: Were there any other aspects of preproduction that you were involved with?

PA: Involved might be too strong a word, but I did have numerous conversations with Kalina Ivanov, the production designer. Particularly about the apartment that Bill Hurt's character lives in. That was the only set constructed for the movie—on a sound stage in Long Island City. Everything else was filmed in real places. Considering that the apartment is lived in by a novelist, it made sense that Kalina should want to consult with me. We talked about everything: the books on the shelves, the pictures on the walls, the precise contents of the clutter on the desk. I think she did a remarkable job. For once, there's an authentic-looking New York apartment in a movie. Have you ever noticed how many supposedly ordinary people in Hollywood films manage to live in three-million-dollar TriBeCa lofts? The apartment that Kalina designed rings true, and a lot of work and thought went into what she did, things that often aren't even visible on screen. The little coffee-cup rings on the table, the postcard of Herman Melville over the desk, the unused word processor sitting in the corner, a thousand and one minute details. . . . Philosophically speaking, production design is a fascinating dicipline. There's a real spiritual component to it. Because what it entails is looking very closely at the world, seeing things as they really are and not as you want them to be, and then recreating them for wholly imaginary and fictitious purposes. Any job that requires you to look that carefully at the world has to be a good job, a job that's good for the soul.

AI: You're beginning to sound like Auggie Wren!

PA: *(Laughs)* Well, Auggie didn't come out of nowhere. He's a part of me—just as much as I'm a part of him.

AI: Once the shooting started, did you go to the set?

PA: Occasionally. Every now and then I'd stop by to see how things were going, especially when they were filming the cigar store scenes, since that set was within walking distance of my house. And I was up in Peekskill for the last three or four days of shooting. But in general I kept myself at a distance. The set was Wayne's territory, and I didn't want to get in his way. He didn't sit in my room with me while I wrote the script, so it seemed only right to do the same for him. . . . What I did do, however, was attend the dailies every evening at the DuArt Building on West 55th Street. That proved to be indispensable. I saw every inch of footage, and when we went into the cutting room in mid-July, I had a pretty good understanding of what the options were. . . . The dailies were also instructive in teaching me how to cope with disappointment. Every time an actor blew a line or strayed from the script, it was like a knife going through my heart. But that's what happens when you collaborate with other people, it's something you have to learn to live with. I'm talking about the smallest deviations from what I wrote, things that only I would notice, probably. But still, you work hard to get the words to scan in a certain way, and it's painful to see them come out in another way. . . . And yet, there's another side to it, too. Sometimes the actors improvised or threw in extra lines, and a number of these additions definitely improved the film. For example, Harvey yelling at the irate customer in the cigar store: "Take it on the arches, you fat fuck!" I'd never heard that expression before, and I found it hilarious. Just the kind of thing Auggie would say. . . .

AI: So, even if you didn't go to the set every day, you were prepared to contribute after the shooting was finished.

PA: I hadn't really planned to get so involved in the editing, but like so many other things connected with *Smoke,* it just seemed to happen on its own. Maysie Hoy had worked with Wayne on his last movie, Wayne and I already knew each other well, and it turned out that Maysie and I hit it off—as if we'd been friends in some previous incarnation. It was an excellent three-way relationship. We all felt free to express our opinions, to talk through every little problem that arose, and each one of us listened carefully to what the other two had to say. The atmosphere was one of respect and equality. No hierarchies, no intellectual terrorism. We worked together for weeks and months, and there was rarely any tension. Hard work, yes, but also a lot of jokes and laughter.

AI: When it comes down to it, that's where every movie is really made. In the cutting room.

PA: It's like starting all over again. You begin with the script, which establishes a certain idea of what the film should be, and then you shoot the script, and things begin to change. The actors' performances bring out different meanings, different shadings, things are lost, other things are found. Then you go into the cutting room and try to marry the script to the performances. At times, the two mesh very harmoniously. At other times, they don't, and that can be maddening. You're stuck with the footage you have, and that limits the possibilities. You're like a novelist trying to revise his book, but fifty percent of the words in the dictionary are not available to you. You're not allowed to use them. . . . So you fiddle and shape and juggle, you search for a rhythm, a musical flow to carry you from one scene to the next, and you have to be willing to discard material, to think in terms of the whole, of what is essential to the overall good of the film. . . . Then, on top of these considerations, there's the question of time. A novel can be ninety pages or nine hundred pages, and no one thinks twice about it. But a movie has to be a certain length, two hours or less. It's a fixed form, like a sonnet, and you have to get everything into that limited space. As it happened, the script I wrote was too long. I cut things from it before we started shooting, but even so, it was still too long. The first assemblage that Maysie put together was two hours and fifty minutes, which meant that we had to cut out almost a third of the story. To tell the truth, I didn't see how it could be done. From what I understand, nearly everyone who makes a movie has to face this problem. That's why it always takes longer to cut a film than to shoot it.

AI: What was the biggest surprise that turned up in the cutting room?

PA: There were many surprises, but the biggest one would have to be the last scene, when Paul tells Auggie the Christmas story. As originally written, the story was supposed to be intercut with black-and-white footage that would illustrate what Auggie was saying. The idea was to go back and forth between the restaurant and Granny Ethel's apartment, and when we weren't watching Auggie tell the story, we would hear his voice over the black-and-white material. When we put it together that way, however, it didn't work. The words and the images clashed. You'd settle into listening to Auggie, and then, when the black-and-white pictures started to roll, you'd get so caught up in the visual information that you'd stop listening to the words. By the time you went back to Auggie's face, you'd have missed a couple of sentences and lost the thread of the story.

We had to think through the whole business from scratch, and what we finally decided to do was keep the two elements separate. Auggie tells his story in the restaurant, and then, as a kind of coda, we see a close-up of Paul's typewriter typing out the last words of the title page of the story Auggie has given him, which then dissolves into the black-and-white footage with the Tom Waits song playing over it. This was the only plausible solution, and I feel it works well. It's a rare thing in movies to watch someone tell a story for ten minutes. The camera is on Harvey's face for almost the whole time, and because Harvey is such a powerful and believable actor, he manages to pull it off. When all is said and done, it's probably the best scene in the film.

AI: The camera moves in very close in that scene, right up against Harvey's mouth. I wasn't expecting that at all.

PA: Wayne worked out the visual language of the film in a very bold and interesting way. All the early scenes are done in wide shots and masters. Then, very gradually, as the disparate characters become more involved with each other, there are more and more close shots and singles. Ninety-nine percent of the people who see the film probably won't notice this. It works in a highly subliminal way, but in relation to the material in the film, to the kind of story we were trying to tell, it was the right approach. By the time we get to the last scene in the restaurant, the camera has apparently moved in on the actors as close as it ever will. A limit has been established, the rules have been defined—and then, suddenly, the camera pushes in even closer, as close as it can get. The viewer is not at all prepared for it. It's as if the camera is bulldozing through a brick wall, breaking down the last barrier against genuine human intimacy. In some way, the emotional resolution of the entire film is contained in that shot.

AI: I like the title of the film, *Smoke*. It's catchy and evocative. Would you care to elaborate?

PA: On the word "smoke"? I'd say it's many things all at once. It refers to the cigar store, of course, but also to the way smoke can obscure things and make them illegible. Smoke is something that is never fixed, that is constantly changing shape. In the same way that the characters in the film keep changing as their lives intersect. Smoke signals . . . smoke screens . . . smoke drifting through the air. In small ways and large ways, each character is continually changed by the other characters around him.

AI: It's hard to pin down the tone of the film. Would you call it a comedy? A drama? Perhaps the French category "dramatic comedy" is more appropriate?

PA: You're probably onto something there. I've always thought of it as a comedy—but in the classical sense of the term, meaning that all the characters in the story are a little better off at the end than they were in the beginning. Not to get too high-flown about it, but when you think about the difference between Shakespeare's comedies and tragedies, it's not so much in the material of the plays as in how the conflicts are resolved. The same kinds of human problems exist in both. With the tragedies, everyone winds up dead on the stage. With the comedies, everyone is still standing and life goes on. That's how I think of *Smoke*. Good things happen, bad things happen, but life goes on. Therefore, it's a comedy. Or, if you prefer, a dramatic comedy.

AI: With some dark spots.

PA: Definitely. That goes without saying. It's not farce or slapstick, but at bottom it takes a fairly optimistic view of the human condition. In many ways, I think the screenplay is the most optimistic thing I've ever written.

AI: It's also one of the very few American films of recent years in which the characters take pleasure in smoking. And there's no one walking into the frame telling them not to do it.

PA: Well, the fact is that people smoke. If I'm not mistaken, more than a billion people light up around the world every day. I know the anti-smoking lobby in this country has grown very strong in the last few years, but Puritanism has always been with us. In one way or another, the teetotalers and zealots have always been a force in American life. I'm not saying that smoking is good for you, but compared to the political and social and ecological outrages committed every day, tobacco is a minor issue. People smoke. That's a fact. People smoke, and they enjoy it, even if it isn't good for them.

AI: You won't get an argument from me.

PA: I'm just guessing now, but maybe all this is connected to the way the characters act in the film . . . to what you might call an undogmatic view of human behavior. Does this sound too far-fetched? I mean, no one is simply one thing or the other. They're all filled with contradictions, and they don't live in a world that breaks down neatly into good guys and bad guys. Each person in the story has his strengths and weaknesses. At his best, for example, Auggie is close to being a Zen master. But he's also an operator, a wise guy, and a downright grumpy son-of-a-bitch. Rashid is essentially a good and very bright kid, but he's also a liar, a thief, and an impudent little prick. Do you see what I'm driving at?

AI: Absolutely. As I said before, you won't get an argument from me.

PA: That's the spirit.

AI: Another question—about Brooklyn. I'd like you to tell me why the film is set there. I know you live in Brooklyn, but was there any special reason—other than familiarity?

PA: I've been living there for fifteen years now, and I must say I'm fond of my neighborhood, Park Slope. It has to be one of the most democratic and tolerant places on the planet. Everyone lives there, every race and religion and economic class, and everyone pretty much gets along. Given the climate in the country today, I would say that qualifies as a miracle. I also know that terrible things go on in Brooklyn, not to speak of New York as a whole. Wrenching things, unbearable things—but by and large the city works. In spite of everything, in spite of all the potential for hatred and violence, most people make an effort to get along with each other most of the time. The rest of the country perceives New York as a hellhole, but that's only one part of the story. I wanted to explore the other side of things in *Smoke,* to work against some of the stereotypes that people carry around about this place.

AI: I'm curious why the novelist in *Smoke* is named Paul. Is there an autobiographical element in the film?

PA: No, not really. The name Paul is a holdover from the Christmas story published in the *Times.* Because the story was going to appear in a newspaper, I wanted to bring reality and fiction as close together as possible, to leave some doubt in the reader's mind as to whether the story was true or not. So I put in my own name to add to the confusion—but only my first name. The writer that Bill Hurt plays in *Smoke* has nothing to do with me. He's an invented character.

AI: Tell me a little about *Blue in the Face.* Not only did you and Wayne make this other film after *Smoke,* but you wound up as co-director.

PA: Weird but true. It's a crazy project that was filmed in a total of six days. We're still in the process of putting it together, so I don't want to say too much about it, but I can give you the rough outline.

AI: Please.

PA: It all started during the rehearsals for *Smoke.* Harvey came in to work on some of the cigar store scenes with the OTB Men—Giancarlo Esposito, José Zuniga, and Steve Gevedon. As a way of warming up and getting to know each other, they launched into a few short improvisations. It turned out to be very funny. Wayne and I just about fell on the floor, and in a burst of enthusiasm he announced: "I think we should make another film with you guys after *Smoke* is finished. Let's go back into the cigar store for a few days and see what happens."

AI: It might have started out with those four, but the cast certainly grew. You had some of the other actors from *Smoke*—Jared Harris, Mel Gorham, Victor Argo, and Malik Yoba—but also Lily Tomlin, Michael J. Fox, Roseanne, Lou Reed, Jim Jarmusch, Mira Sorvino, Keith David, and Madonna. Not too shabby.

PA: No, not too shabby. Everyone worked for scale—with the best spirit in the world. They were all troopers, every last one of them.

AI: And you did it with no script?

PA: No script—and no rehearsals. I wrote out notes for all the scenes and situations, so each actor more or less knew what had to be done, but there was no script per se, no written dialogue. . . . It was shot in two stages: three days in mid-July and three days in late October. It was wild, let me tell you, pure chaos from start to finish.

AI: And fun.

PA: Oh yes, lots of fun. I enjoyed myself immensely. The finished film is sure to be one of the oddest films ever made: wall-to-wall wackiness, a lighter-than-air creampuff, an hour and a half of singing, dancing, and loopy shenanigans. It's a hymn to the great People's Republic of Brooklyn, and a cruder, more vulgar piece of work would be hard to imagine. Strangely enough, it appears to work well with *Smoke*. They're opposite sides of the same coin, I guess, and the two films seem to complement each other in mysterious ways.

AI: Now that you've caught the bug, do you have any desire to direct again?

PA: No, I can't say that I do. Working on these films has been a terrific experience, and I'm glad it happened, I'm glad I got caught up in it as fully as I did. But enough is enough. It's time for me to crawl back into my hole and begin writing again. There's a new novel calling out to be written, and I can't wait to lock myself in my room and get started.

November 22, 1994

smoke

Directed by **Wayne Wang**
Written by **Paul Auster**
Produced by **Greg Johnson, Peter Newman,**
Kenzo Harikoshi, and Hisami Kuroiwa
Director of Photography **Adam Holender**
Editor **Maysie Hoy**
Production Designer **Kalina Ivanov**
Line Producer **Diana Phillips**
Costumes **Claudia Brown**
Music **Rachel Portman**
Executive Producers **Bob Weinstein, Harvey Weinstein,**
and Satoru Iseki
Still Photographer **Lorey Sebastian**

Cast
(In order of appearance)
Auggie Wren **Harvey Keitel**
Tommy **Giancarlo Esposito**
Jerry **José Zuniga**
Dennis **Steve Gevedon**
Jimmy Rose **Jared Harris**
Paul Benjamin **William Hurt**
Book Thief **Daniel Auster**
Rashid Cole **Harold Perrineau, Jr.**
Waitress **Deirdre O'Connell**
Vinnie **Victor Argo**
Aunt Em **Michelle Hurst**
Cyrus Cole **Forest Whitaker**
Ruby McNutt **Stockard Channing**
Irate Customer **Vincenzo Amelia**
Doreen Cole **Erica Gimpel**
Cyrus, Jr. **Gilson Reglas**
Baseball Announcer **Howie Rose**
Felicity **Ashley Judd**

April Lee **Mary Ward**
Violet **Mel Gorham**
1st Lawyer **Baxter Harris**
2nd Lawyer **Paul Geier**
Charles Clemm (The Creeper) **Malik Yoba**
Roger Goodwin **Walter T. Mead**
Waiter **Murray Moston**
Granny Ethel **Clarice Taylor**

1. EXT: DAY. ELEVATED SUBWAY TRAIN

Against the backdrop of the Manhattan skyline, we see an elevated sub-way train heading toward Brooklyn.

After a moment, we begin to hear voices. An animated discussion is tak-ing place inside the Brooklyn Cigar Company.

2. INT: DAY. THE BROOKLYN CIGAR CO.

The cigar shop from within. Displays of cigar boxes, a wall of magazines, piles of newspapers, cigarettes, smoking paraphernalia. On the walls, we see framed black-and-white photographs of people smoking cigars: Groucho Marx, George Burns, Clint Eastwood, Edward G. Robinson, Orson Welles, Charles Laughton, Frankenstein's monster, Leslie Caron, Ernie Kovacs.

Words appear on the screen: "SUMMER 1990."

AUGGIE WREN is behind the counter. Somewhere between forty and fifty years old, AUGGIE is a scruffy presence: unkempt hair, a two-day stubble of beard, dressed in blue jeans and a black T-shirt. We see an intricate tat-too on one arm.

It is a slow hour. AUGGIE is flipping through a photography magazine.

Near the counter are the three OTB MEN. These are local characters who like to hang out in the store, shooting the breeze with AUGGIE. One is black (TOMMY) and the other two are white (JERRY and DENNIS). DENNIS wears a T-shirt with the following words printed across the front: "If life is a dream, what happens when I wake up?"

TOMMY

I'll tell you why they're not going anywhere.

JERRY

Yeah? And why is that?

TOMMY

Management. Those guys are walking around with their heads up their asses.

DENNIS

They made some great deals, Tommy. Hernandez, Carter. Without those two, there never woulda been no World Series.

TOMMY

That was four years ago. I'm talking about now. *(Growing more intense)* Look who they got rid of. Mitchell. Backman. McDowell. Dykstra. Aguillera. Mookie. Mookie Wilson, for Chrissakes. *(Shakes his head)*

JERRY

(Sarcastically) And Nolan Ryan. Don't forget him.

DENNIS

(Chiming in) Yeah. And Amos Otis.

TOMMY

(Shrugs) Okay, joke about it. I don't give a shit.

JERRY

Jesus, Tommy, it ain't science, you know. You got your good trades and your bad trades. That's how it works.

TOMMY

They didn't have to do a thing, that's all I'm saying. The team was good, the best fucking team in baseball. But then they had to screw it up.

(Pause) They traded their birthright for a mess of porridge. *(Shakes his head)* A mess of porridge.

The bells on the door jangle as someone enters. It is AUGGIE'S protégé, JIMMY ROSE, a mentally retarded man in his late twenties. He has been sweeping the sidewalk outside the store and holds a broom in his right hand.

                         AUGGIE
How'd you do out there, Jimmy?

                         JIMMY
Good, Auggie. Real good. *(Proudly thrusts out broom)* All finished.

                         AUGGIE
(Philosophically) It'll never be finished.

                         JIMMY
(Confused) Huh?

                         AUGGIE
That's how it is with sidewalks. People come, people go, and they all drop shit on the ground. As soon as you clean up one spot and move on to the next, the first spot is dirty again.

                         JIMMY
(Trying to digest AUGGIE'S comment) I just do what you tell me, Auggie. You tell me to sweep, so I sweep.

The bells on the door jangle again, and a customer enters the store: a middle-class man in his early thirties. He walks to the counter as JERRY teases JIMMY. In the background, we see him talking to AUGGIE. AUGGIE pulls some cigar boxes out of the display case and puts them on the counter for the YOUNG MAN to inspect. In the foreground we see:

                         JERRY
(Interrupting. Playfully) Hey, Jimmy. You got the time?

                         JIMMY
(Turning to the SECOND OTB MAN) Huh?

JERRY

You still have that watch Auggie gave you?

JIMMY

(Holds up left wrist, showing cheap digital watch. Smiles) Tick-tock, tick-tock.

JERRY

So what's the time?

JIMMY

(Studying watch) Twelve-eleven. *(Pause, marvelling as the numbers change)* Twelve-twelve. *(Looks up, smiling)* Twelve-twelve.

A sudden outburst is heard from the area near the counter.

YOUNG MAN

(Aghast) Ninety-two dollars?

The focus of the scene shifts to AUGGIE and the YOUNG MAN.

AUGGIE

They don't come cheap, son. These little honeys are works of art. Rolled by hand in a tropical climate, most likely by an eighteen-year-old girl in a thin cotton dress with no underwear on. Little beads of sweat forming in her naked cleavage. The smooth, delicate fingers nimbly turning out one masterpiece after another. . . .

YOUNG MAN

(Pointing) And how much are these?

AUGGIE

Seventy-eight dollars. The girl who rolled these was probably wearing panties.

YOUNG MAN

(Pointing) And these?

AUGGIE

Fifty-six. That girl had on a corset.

YOUNG MAN

(Pointing) And these?

AUGGIE

Forty-four. They're on special this week from the Canary Islands. A real bargain.

YOUNG MAN

I think I'll take them. *(Takes wallet from his pocket and counts out $50— which he hands to AUGGIE)*

AUGGIE

A good choice. You wouldn't want to celebrate the birth of your firstborn with a box of stinkers, would you? Remember to keep them in the refrigerator until you hand them out.

YOUNG MAN

The refrigerator?

AUGGIE

It'll keep them fresh. If they get too dry, they'll break. And you don't want that to happen, do you? *(Putting cigar box into a bag, ringing up sale on the cash register)* Tobacco is a plant, and it needs the same loving care you'd give an orchid.

YOUNG MAN

Thanks for the tip.

AUGGIE

Any time. And congratulations to you and your wife. Just remember, though, in the immortal words of Rudyard Kipling: "A woman is just a woman, but a cigar is a smoke."

YOUNG MAN

(Confused) What does that mean?

AUGGIE

Damned if I know. But it has a nice ring to it, don't it?

At that moment, we hear the bells on the door jangle again. Cut to the door. Another customer enters the store: PAUL BENJAMIN. He is in his early forties, dressed in rumpled casual clothes. As he approaches the counter, the YOUNG MAN brushes past him and leaves the store. The OTB MEN and JIMMY look on as PAUL and AUGGIE talk.

PAUL

Hey, Auggie. How's it going?

AUGGIE

Hey, man. Good to see you. What'll it be today?

PAUL

Two tins of Schimmelpennincks. And throw in a lighter while you're at it.

AUGGIE

(Reaching for cigars and lighter) The boys and I were just having a philosophical discussion about women and cigars. Some interesting connections there, don't you think?

PAUL

(Laughs) Definitely. *(Pause)* I suppose it all goes back to Queen Elizabeth.

AUGGIE

The Queen of England?

PAUL

Not Elizabeth the Second, Elizabeth the First. (Pause) Did you ever hear of Sir Walter Raleigh?

TOMMY

Sure. He's the guy who threw his cloak down over the puddle.

JERRY

I used to smoke Raleigh cigarettes. They came with a free gift coupon in every pack.

PAUL

That's the man. Well, Raleigh was the person who introduced tobacco in England, and since he was a favorite of the Queen's—Queen Bess, he used to call her—smoking caught on as a fashion at court. I'm sure Old Bess must have shared a stogie or two with Sir Walter. Once, he made a bet with her that he could measure the weight of smoke.

DENNIS

You mean, weigh smoke?

PAUL

Exactly. Weigh smoke.

TOMMY

You can't do that. It's like weighing air.

PAUL

I admit it's strange. Almost like weighing someone's soul. But Sir Walter was a clever guy. First, he took an unsmoked cigar and put it on a balance and weighed it. Then he lit up and smoked the cigar, carefully tapping the ashes into the balance pan. When he was finished, he put the butt into the pan along with the ashes and weighed what was there. Then he subtracted that number from the original weight of the unsmoked cigar. The difference was the weight of the smoke.

TOMMY

Not bad. That's the kind of guy we need to take over the Mets.

PAUL

Oh, he was smart, all right. But not so smart that he didn't wind up having his head chopped off twenty years later. *(Pause)* But that's another story.

AUGGIE

(Handing PAUL his change and putting cigar tins and lighter in a paper bag) Seven eighty-five out of twenty. *(As PAUL turns to leave)* Take care of yourself now, and don't do anything I wouldn't do.

PAUL

(Smiling) I wouldn't think of it. *(Waves casually to the OTB MEN)* See you around, fellas.

AUGGIE *and the* OTB MEN *watch as PAUL leaves the store.*

TOMMY

(Turning to AUGGIE) What is he, some kind of wise guy?

AUGGIE

Nah. He's a good kid.

JERRY

I've seen him around. He comes in here a lot, don't he?

AUGGIE

Couple of times a week, maybe. He's a writer. Lives in the neighborhood.

TOMMY

And what kind of writer is he? An underwriter?

AUGGIE

(Peeved) Very funny. Some of the cracks you make, Tommy, sometimes I think you should see a doctor. You know, go in for some wit therapy or something. To clean out the valves in your brain.

TOMMY

(A little embarrassed. Shrugs) It was just a joke.

AUGGIE

The guy's a novelist. Paul Benjamin. You ever hear of him? *(Pause)* That's a stupid question. The only things you guys read is the *Racing Form* and the sports pages of the *Post. (Pause)* He's published three or four books. But nothing now for the past few years.

DENNIS

What's the matter? He run out of ideas?

AUGGIE

He ran out of luck. *(Pause)* Remember that holdup out here on Seventh Avenue a few years back?

JERRY

You talking about the bank? The time those two guys started spraying bullets all over the street?

AUGGIE

That's it. Four people got killed. One of them was Paul's wife. *(Pause)* The poor lug, he hasn't been the same since. *(Pause)* The funny thing was, she stopped in here just before it happened. To stock up on cigars for him. She was a nice lady, Ellen. Four or five months pregnant at the time, which means that when she was killed, the baby was killed, too.

TOMMY

Bad day at Black Rock, eh, Auggie?

Close-up of AUGGIE'S face. Remembering.

AUGGIE

It was bad, all right. I sometimes think that if she hadn't given me exact change that day, or if the store had been a little more crowded, it would have taken her a few more seconds to get out of here, and then maybe she wouldn't have stepped in front of that bullet. She'd still be alive, the baby would have been born, and Paul would be sitting at home writing another book instead of wandering the streets with a hangover. *(Pensive. His expression suddenly turns to one of alarm)*

Cut to white youth in the corner of the store, shoving paperback books into the pockets of his tattered army fatigue jacket.

AUGGIE (cont'd)

Hey! What are you doing there, kid? Hey, cut that out!

AUGGIE *scrambles out from behind the counter, pushing his way past the* OTB MEN *as the kid takes off and runs out of the store.*

3. EXT: DAY. SEVENTH AVENUE

AUGGIE *chases the* BOOK THIEF *down the street. Eventually, he gets wind-ed and gives up. He pauses for a moment to catch his breath, then turns around and heads back in the direction of the store.*

4. INT: DAY. PAUL'S APARTMENT. A BROWNSTONE BUILDING IN PARK SLOPE (THIRD FLOOR)

Shot of a little brown cigar, burning in an ashtray.

The camera pulls back to reveal PAUL *at his desk. He is writing in long-hand, using a pad of yellow legal paper. An old Smith-Corona typewriter is also on the desk, poised for work with a half-written page in the roller. Off in the corner, we see a neglected word processor.*

The workroom is a bare and simple place. Desk, chair, and a small wood-en bookcase with manuscripts and papers shoved onto its shelves. The window faces a brick wall.

As PAUL *continues to write, the camera travels from the workroom into the larger of the two rooms that make up his apartment.*

This larger room is an all-purpose space that includes a sleeping area, a kitchenette in one corner, a dining table, and a large easy chair. Crowded bookshelves occupy one wall from floor to ceiling. The bow win-dows face front, looking down onto the street. Near the bed, we see a framed photograph of a young woman. (This is Ellen, Paul's dead wife.)

The camera travels back into the workroom. We see PAUL *at work. Fade out.*

Fade in. We see PAUL *at his desk, eating a TV dinner while still writing in* the pad. After a moment, he inadvertently knocks the food off the desk with his elbow. He begins to bend over to pick up the food, but as he does so a new idea suddenly occurs to him. Instead of cleaning up the mess, he turns back to his pad and continues writing.

5. EXT: DAY. IN FRONT OF THE BROOKLYN CIGAR CO.

We see PAUL walking out of the cigar store. JIMMY ROSE is on the corner, observing him throughout the scene. PAUL takes three or four steps, then realizes he has forgotten something. He goes back into the store. During his brief absence, JIMMY remains on the corner, imitating PAUL'S gestures: patting in pockets, looking puzzled, realizing that he has forgotten the cigars he just bought.

PAUL comes out again a moment later, holding a tin of Schimmelpenninck cigars. He pauses, takes a cigar out of the tin, and lights up. He continues walking, obviously distracted. He stops briefly at a corner, then steps out into the street, paying no attention to the traffic. A speeding tow truck is rushing toward the intersection. At the last second, a black hand reaches out, grabs PAUL by the arm, and pulls him back to the curb. If not for that timely move, PAUL would surely have been run down.

We see PAUL'S rescuer: it is RASHID COLE, a black adolescent of sixteen or seventeen. He is tall and well built for his age. A nylon backpack is slung over his left shoulder.

RASHID
Watch out, man. You'll get yourself killed like that.

PAUL
(Badly shaken, still clinging to RASHID'S arm) I can't believe I did that . . . Christ, I'm walking around in a fog . . .

RASHID
No harm done. Everything's okay now. (Looks down and notices that he and PAUL are still gripping each other's arms. Tries to pull away) I've got to be going.

PAUL

(Still rattled. Begins to loosen grip, then grabs hold of RASHID'S arm again) No, wait. You can't just walk off. *(Pause)* You saved my life.

RASHID

(Shrugs) I just happened to be there. The right place at the right time.

PAUL

(Relaxing grip on RASHID'S arm) I owe you something.

RASHID

It's okay, mister. No big deal.

PAUL

Yes it is. It's a law of the universe. If I let you walk away, the moon will spin out of orbit . . . pestilence will reign over the city for a hundred years.

RASHID

(Mystified, amused. Smiles faintly) Well, if you put it that way . . .

PAUL

You have to let me do something for you to put the scales in balance.

RASHID

(Thinks, shakes his head) That's all right. If I think of something, I'll send
my butler over to tell you.

PAUL

Come on. At least let me buy you a cup of coffee.

RASHID

I don't drink coffee. (Smiles) On the other hand, since you insist, if you
offered me a cold lemonade, I wouldn't say no.

PAUL

Good. Lemonade it is. (Pause. Extends right hand) I'm Paul.

RASHID

Rashid. Rashid Cole. (Shakes PAUL'S hand)

Cut to:

6. INT: DAY. GREEK DINER IN PARK SLOPE

PAUL and RASHID are sitting in a booth. The restaurant is nearly empty.
We see RASHID finishing his second lemonade.

PAUL

(Watching RASHID drink) Are you sure you don't want some food to go
along with it? It might help to absorb some of that liquid. You don't want
to slosh around too much when you stand up.

RASHID

That's okay. I've already had lunch.

PAUL

(Looks at clock on wall) You must eat lunch pretty early. It's only eleven
o'clock.

RASHID

I mean breakfast.

PAUL

(*Studying* RASHID *closely*) Yeah, sure, and I bet you had lobster last night. Along with two bottles of champagne.

RASHID

Just one bottle. I believe in moderation.

PAUL

Look, kid, it's okay with me. You don't have to play games. If you want a hamburger or something, go ahead and order it.

RASHID

(*Hesitates*) Well, maybe just one. To be polite.

PAUL

(*Turning to* WAITRESS. *She comes*) Cocktail hour is over. The young man would like to order a hamburger.

WAITRESS

(*To* RASHID) How do you want that cooked?

RASHID

Medium rare, please.

WAITRESS

Fries?

RASHID

(*Looks at* PAUL. PAUL *nods*) Yes, please.

WAITRESS

Lettuce and tomato?

RASHID

(*Looks at* PAUL. PAUL *nods*) Yes, please.

WAITRESS

(*Pointing to* RASHID'S *empty lemonade glass*) You want another one of these, too?

PAUL

Yeah, give him another one. And I'll take a cup of coffee while you're at it.

WAITRESS

Hot coffee or iced coffee?

PAUL

Do you have real iced coffee, or do you just pour hot coffee over some ice cubes?

WAITRESS

Everything is real in here, honey. *(Pause)* As real as the color of my hair.

PAUL *and* RASHID *look at her hair. It is dyed bright red.*

PAUL

(Deadpan) I'll take the iced coffee. *(Pause)* You only live once, right?

WAITRESS

(Equally deadpan) If you're lucky. *(Pause)* Then again, it depends on what you call living. *(She walks off)*

PAUL

(To RASHID) I don't mean to pry, but I see a kid walking around with a big knapsack on his back, and I begin to wonder if all his worldly possessions aren't stowed in there. Are you in some kind of trouble or what?

RASHID

(Keeping up his pose) Mostly what.

PAUL

(Studying RASHID) You don't have to tell me if you don't want to, but I might be able to help.

RASHID

(Hesitating) You don't know me from a hole in the wall.

PAUL

That's true. But I also owe you something, and I'm not sure that buying you a hamburger is going to do the job. *(Pause)* What is it? Family problems? Money problems?

RASHID

(Imitating white upper-class accent) Oh no, Momsie and Popsie have oodles.

PAUL

And where do Momsie and Popsie live?

RASHID

East Seventy-fourth Street.

PAUL

In Manhattan?

RASHID

Of course. Where else?

PAUL

Then what are you doing in Park Slope? It's a little far from home, isn't it?

RASHID

(Beginning to relent) That's where the *what* comes in.

PAUL

The what?

RASHID

The what. *(Pause)* I've kind of run away from home, you see. *(Pause)* It has nothing to do with my parents or money. I saw something I wasn't supposed to see, and for the time being it's best that I keep myself out of sight.

PAUL

You can't be more specific than that?

RASHID *looks at* PAUL, *hesitates, then lowers his eyes.*

PAUL (cont'd)

(Pause. Decides not to press him) So where have you been staying in the meantime?

RASHID

Here and there. Around.

PAUL

Uh-huh. One of those cozy bed and breakfast places, probably.

RASHID

Yeah, that's right.

PAUL

Except that there's no bed, is there? And no breakfast either.

RASHID

The material world is an illusion. It doesn't matter if they're there or not. The world is in my head.

PAUL

But your body is in the world, isn't it? *(Pause)* If someone offered you a place to stay, you wouldn't necessarily refuse, would you?

RASHID

(Pause. Thinks) People don't do that kind of thing. Not in New York.

PAUL

I'm not "people." I'm just me. And I do whatever I goddamn want to do. Got it?

RASHID

Thanks, but I'll manage.

PAUL

In case you're wondering, I like women, not little boys. And I'm not offering you a long-term lease—just a place to crash for a couple of nights.

RASHID

I can take care of myself. Don't worry.

PAUL

Suit yourself. But if you change your mind, here's the address. *(Takes out a pad from his pocket and scribbles down the address. Tears sheet from the pad and hands it to RASHID)*

The WAITRESS arrives with their orders.

WAITRESS

One burger medium rare with lettuce and tomato. *(Setting down plate in front of RASHID)* One order of fries. *(Setting down plate)* One lemonade. *(Setting down glass)* And one dose of reality. *(Setting down iced coffee in front of PAUL)*

PAUL *looks on as* RASHID *picks up hamburger and takes his first bite.*

7. INT: DAY. THE BROOKLYN CIGAR CO.

A slow hour. AUGGIE *is sitting behind the counter, looking through a magazine and eating a slice of pizza for lunch.* VINNIE *enters the frame. He is the owner of the store: a large man in his fifties.*

VINNIE

Okay, I think everything's set. *(Lights up cigar)* You've got the number for Cape Cod, right? Just in case something goes wrong.

AUGGIE

(Chewing pizza, not looking up from magazine) No problem, Vinnie. Everything's under control. *(Finally looking up)* I could run this store in my sleep.

VINNIE

(Studying AUGGIE) How long you been working for me, Auggie?

AUGGIE

(Shrugs, looks down at magazine again) I don't know. Thirteen, fourteen years. Something like that.

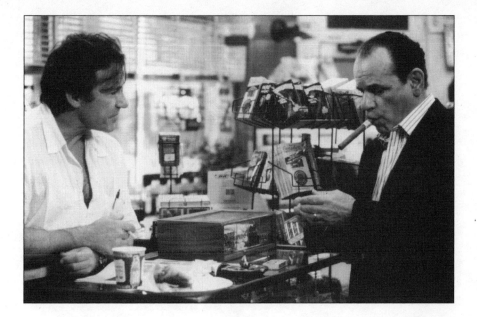

VINNIE

It's pretty crazy, don't you think? I mean, a smart guy like you. What do you want to hang on to a dead-end job like this for?

AUGGIE

(Shrugs again) I don't know. *(Turns pages of magazine)* Maybe because I love you so much, boss.

VINNIE

Shit. You should have been married to someone by now. You know, settled down somewhere with a kid or two, a nice steady job.

AUGGIE

I almost got married once.

VINNIE

Yeah, I know. To that girl who moved to Pittsburgh.

AUGGIE

Ruby McNutt. My one true love.

VINNIE

Sounds like another one of your stories to me.

AUGGIE

(Shakes his head) She upped and married some other cat after I joined the navy. By the time I got my discharge, though, she was divorced. Her husband poked out her eye in a domestic quarrel.

VINNIE

(Puffing on his cigar) Lovely.

AUGGIE

(Remembering) She made a play for me after I got back, but her glass eye kept interfering with my concentration. Every time we got into a clinch, I'd start thinking about that hole in her head, that empty socket with the glass eye in it. An eye that couldn't see, an eye that couldn't shed any tears. The minute I started thinking about it, Mr. Johnson would get all soft and small. And I can't see getting married if Mr. Johnson isn't going to be in tiptop shape.

VINNIE

(Shaking his head) You don't take anything seriously, do you?

AUGGIE

I try not to, anyway. It's better for your health. I mean, look at you, Vincent. You're the guy with the wife and three kids and the ranch house on Long Island. You're the guy with the white shoes and the white Caddy and the white shag carpet. But you've had two heart attacks, and I'm still waiting for my first.

VINNIE

(Takes cigar out of his mouth and looks at it with disgust) I should stop smoking these damn things is what I should do. The fuckers are going to kill me one day.

AUGGIE

Enjoy it while you can, Vin. Pretty soon, they're going to legislate us out of business anyway.

VINNIE

They catch you smoking tobacco, they'll stand you up against a wall and shoot you.

AUGGIE

(Nodding) Tobacco today, sex tomorrow. In three or four years, it'll probably be against the law to smile at strangers.

VINNIE

(Remembering something) Speaking of which, are you still going ahead with that deal on the Montecristos?

AUGGIE

It's all set. My guy in Miami said he'd have them within the next few weeks. (Pause) Are you sure you don't want to go in with me? Five thousand dollars outlay, a guaranteed ten-thousand-dollar return. A consortium of Court Street lawyers and judges. They're just drooling to get their lips around some genuine Cuban cigars.

VINNIE

No thanks. I don't care what you do, but just make sure you don't get caught, okay? The last I heard, it was still illegal to sell Cuban cigars in this country.

AUGGIE

It's the law that's buying. That's what's so beautiful about it. I mean, when was the last time you heard of a judge sending himself to jail?

VINNIE

Suit yourself. But don't keep the boxes around here long.

AUGGIE

They come in, they go out. I've got it planned to the last detail.

VINNIE

(Looking at his watch) I've got to get moving. Terry will bust my chops if I'm late. See you in September, Auggie.

AUGGIE

Okay, my man. Love to the wife and kids, et cetera, et cetera. Drop me a postcard if you can remember the address.

VINNIE leaves. AUGGIE turns back to his pizza and magazine.

8. EXT: EVENING. FACADE OF THE BROOKLYN CIGAR CO.

A shot of the darkening sky. A shot of the cigar store. We see the lights go out. AUGGIE comes outside, locks the door, and begins pulling down the metal gate in front of the windows. Cut to:

A shot of PAUL running down the street toward AUGGIE.

> PAUL
>
> *(Out of breath)* Are you closed?

> AUGGIE
>
> You run out of Schimmelpennincks?

> PAUL
>
> *(Nods)* Do you think I could buy some before you leave?

> AUGGIE
>
> No problem. It's not as though I'm rushing off to the opera or anything.

AUGGIE lifts the gate and the two of them go into the store.

9. INT: EVENING. THE BROOKLYN CIGAR CO.

PAUL *and* AUGGIE *enter the darkened store.* AUGGIE *turns on the lights and then goes behind the counter to fetch* PAUL'S *cigars.* PAUL, *on the other side, notices a 35-millimeter camera near the cash register.*

                              PAUL
Looks like someone forgot a camera.

                              AUGGIE
(Turning around) Yeah, I did.

                              PAUL
It's yours?

                              AUGGIE
It's mine all right. I've owned that little sucker for a long time.

                              PAUL
I didn't know you took pictures.

                              AUGGIE
(Handing PAUL *his cigars)* I guess you could call it a hobby. It doesn't take me more than about five minutes a day to do it, but I do it every day. Rain or shine, sleet or snow. Sort of like the postman. *(Pause)* Sometimes it feels like my hobby is my real job, and my job is just a way to support my hobby.

                              PAUL
So you're not just some guy who pushes coins across a counter.

                              AUGGIE
That's what people see, but that ain't necessarily what I am.

                              PAUL
(Looking at AUGGIE *with new eyes)* How'd you get started?

                              AUGGIE
Taking pictures? *(Smiles)* It's a long story. I'd need two or three drinks to get through that one.

PAUL

(Nodding) A photographer . . .

AUGGIE

Well, let's not exaggerate. I take pictures. You line up what you want in the viewfinder and click the shutter. No need to mess around with all that artisto crap.

PAUL

I'd like to see your pictures some day.

AUGGIE

It can be arranged. Seeing as how I've read your books, I don't see why I shouldn't share my pictures with you. (Pause. Suddenly embarrassed) It would be an honor.

10. INT: NIGHT. AUGGIE'S APARTMENT

AUGGIE and PAUL are sitting at the kitchen table, opened boxes of Chinese food pushed to one side. Most of the surface of the table is covered with large black photograph albums. There are fourteen in all, and the spine of each one is labelled with a year—ranging from 1977 to 1990. One of these albums (1987) is open on PAUL's lap.

Close-up of one of the pages in the album. There are six black-and-white photos on the page, each one of an identical scene: the corner of 3rd Street and Seventh Avenue at eight o'clock in the morning. In the upper-right-hand corner of each photo, there is a small white label bearing the date: 8-9-87, 8-10-87, 8-11-87, etc. PAUL's hand turns the page; we see six more similar photographs. He turns the page again: same thing. And again: same thing.

PAUL

(Astonished) They're all the same.

AUGGIE

(Smiling proudly) That's right. More than four thousand pictures of the same place. The corner of Third Street and Seventh Avenue at eight

o'clock in the morning. Four thousand straight days in all kinds of weather. *(Pause)* That's why I can never take a vacation. I've got to be in my spot every morning. Every morning in the same spot at the same time.

PAUL

(At a loss. Turns a page, then another page) I've never seen anything like it.

AUGGIE

It's my project. What you'd call my life's work.

PAUL

(Puts down the album and picks up another. Flips through the pages and finds more of the same. Shakes his head in bafflement) Amazing. *(Trying to be polite)* I'm not sure I get it, though. I mean, how did you ever come up with the idea to do this . . . this project?

AUGGIE

I don't know, it just came to me. It's my corner, after all. It's just one little part of the world, but things happen there, too, just like everywhere else. It's a record of my little spot.

PAUL

(*Flipping through the album, still shaking his head*) It's kind of overwhelming.

AUGGIE

(*Still smiling*) You'll never get it if you don't slow down, my friend.

PAUL

What do you mean?

AUGGIE

I mean, you're going too fast. You're hardly even looking at the pictures.

PAUL

But they're all the same.

AUGGIE

They're all the same, but each one is different from every other one. You've got your bright mornings and your dark mornings. You've got your summer light and your autumn light. You've got your weekdays and your weekends. You've got your people in overcoats and galoshes, and you've got your people in shorts and T-shirts. Sometimes the same people, sometimes different ones. And sometimes the different ones become the same, and the same ones disappear. The earth revolves around the sun, and every day the light from the sun hits the earth at a different angle.

PAUL

(Looking up from the album at AUGGIE) Slow down, huh?

AUGGIE

Yeah, that's what I'd recommend. You know how it is. Tomorrow and tomorrow and tomorrow, time creeps on its petty pace.

Close-ups of the photo album. One by one, a single picture occupies the entire screen. AUGGIE'S project unfolds before us. One picture follows another: the same place at the same time at different moments of the year. Close-ups of different faces within the close-ups. The same people appear in different pictures, sometimes looking into the camera, sometimes looking away. Dozens of stills. Finally, we come to a close-up of Ellen, PAUL'S dead wife.

Close-up of PAUL'S face.

PAUL

Jesus, look. It's Ellen.

The camera pulls away. AUGGIE leans over PAUL'S shoulder. We see PAUL'S finger pointing to Ellen's face.

Yeah. There she is. She's in quite a few from that year. She must have been on her way to work.

PAUL

(Moved, on the point of tears) It's Ellen. Look at her. Look at my sweet darling.

Fade out.

11. INT: NIGHT. PAUL'S APARTMENT

We see PAUL scribbling furiously in his legal pad, lost in his work. Behind him, we see ten or twelve index cards pinned to the wall. The cards are covered with writing. One of them reads: "The woman with brown hair and blue eyes." Another one reads: "The mind is led on, step by step, to defeat its own logic." A third one reads: "Remember the Alamo."

PAUL stands up from his desk, goes over to the wall, pulls off one of the cards, and studies it as he returns to his desk. An instant later, he begins writing again.

The intercom buzzer rings loudly in the other room. PAUL continues to work, oblivious to the noise. The buzzer sounds again. PAUL puts down his pen.

PAUL

(Under his breath) Shit. (He stands up from his chair, walks to the other room, and presses the "talk" button on the intercom) Who is it?

VOICE FROM THE INTERCOM

Rashid.

PAUL

Who?

VOICE FROM THE INTERCOM

Rashid Cole. The lemonade kid, remember?

PAUL

Oh, yeah. *(Without much enthusiasm)* Come on up. *(Pushes "door" button on the intercom)*

PAUL *walks to the door and opens it, peering into the hall as he waits for* RASHID *to arrive. A moment later,* RASHID *appears—dressed as before, with the backpack slung over his shoulder. He appears awkward, ill at ease.*

PAUL

I didn't expect to see you again.

RASHID

(Making the best of it) Same here. But I had a long talk with my accountant this afternoon. You know, to see how a move like this would affect my tax picture, and he said it would be okay.

PAUL *studies him with a mixture of bafflement and curiosity, but doesn't answer.* RASHID *puts down his bag and begins looking around the apartment. After a moment:*

PAUL

That's it. Just the two rooms.

RASHID

(Continuing to study his new surroundings) This is the first house I've been in without a TV.

PAUL

I used to have one, but it broke a couple of years ago and I never got around to replacing it. *(Pause)* I'd just as soon not have one anyway. I hate those damn things.

RASHID

But then you don't get to watch the ball games. You told me you were a Mets fan.

PAUL

I listen on the radio. I can see the games just fine that way. *(Pause)* The world is in your head, remember?

RASHID

(Smiles. Continues to walk around. Sees a small pen-and-ink drawing hanging on the wall above the stereo cabinet: the head of a small child. He stops to examine it) Nice drawing. Did you do that?

PAUL

My father did. Believe it or not, that little baby is me.

RASHID

(Studying the drawing more carefully. Turns to look at PAUL, then turns back to the drawing) Yeah, I can believe it.

PAUL

It's strange, though, isn't it? Looking at yourself before you knew who you were.

RASHID

Is your father an artist?

PAUL

No, he was a schoolteacher. But he liked to dabble.

RASHID

He's dead?

PAUL

Twelve, thirteen years ago. (Pause) Actually, he died with his sketch pad open on his lap. Up in the Berkshires one weekend, drawing a picture of Mount Greylock.

RASHID

(Studying the picture, nodding his head. As if to himself) Drawing's a good thing.

PAUL

Is that what you do? Draw pictures?

RASHID

(Smiles) Yeah, sometimes. (Shrugs, as if suddenly embarrassed) I like to dabble, too.

12. INT: DAY. PAUL'S APARTMENT

Two hours later. We see PAUL writing at his desk in the workroom. After a moment, he stands up and opens the double doors a crack. From PAUL'S POV: we see RASHID sitting at the table in the main room, head resting on his arms, asleep. The backpack is still where he put it down in the previous scene.

13. INT: DAY. PAUL'S APARTMENT

8:00 in the morning. PAUL is sitting at the dining table drinking coffee. He looks at his watch, puts down the cup, walks to the workroom door, opens it, pokes head inside. Shot of RASHID asleep on the floor; shot of the typewriter and legal pad on the desk. PAUL closes the door, sighs, returns to the other room and pours himself another cup of coffee. Looks at his watch. Close-up of the watch: dissolve from 8:05 to 8:35. PAUL puts down the cup, stands up, walks to the workroom door, knocks.

                              PAUL
Time to wake up. *(Waits, listens, knocks again)* Hey, kid, time to wake up. *(Waits, listens, knocks again)* Rashid! *(Opens door. RASHID is groggily opening his eyes)* Up and out, I have to work in here. The slumber party is over.

                             RASHID
(Sitting up, rubbing his eyes) What time is it?

                              PAUL
Eight-thirty.

                             RASHID
(Groans, appalled by early hour) Eight-thirty?

                              PAUL
You'll find juice and eggs and milk in the refrigerator. Cereal in the cupboard. Coffee on the stove. Take whatever you want. But it's time for me to get started in here.

RASHID stands up, embarrassed. He is dressed in underpants only. He rolls up the sleeping bag and pushes it to one side. Then he gathers up his clothes and hustles out of the room.

14. INT: DAY. PAUL'S APARTMENT

Twenty minutes later. PAUL is sitting at his desk, staring at his typewriter. A loud noise comes from the other room: the clatter of dishes being put into the sink. PAUL stands up, walks to the door, opens it. He sees RASHID, now fully dressed, picking up the telephone next to the bed. He sees RASHID'S knapsack opened; a brown paper bag is sitting next to it. He watches RASHID dial a number.

                              RASHID
(In a low voice) May I speak to Emily Vail, please? Yes, thank you, I'll wait. (Silence, three or four beats. RASHID fiddles with a pillow on the bed) Aunt Em? Hi, it's me. I just wanted you to know I'm okay. (Pause, as he listens. The response from the other end is an angry one) I know, I'm sorry. (Pause, as he listens) I just didn't want you to worry about me. (Silence, as he listens. Begins to show irritation with Aunt Em's hostility) Just cool it, okay? Take it easy. (Click on the other end. He stares at the receiver for a moment, then hangs up)

PAUL closes the door quietly. RASHID does not know he has been observed. Cut back to PAUL in workroom. He sits down at his desk, thinks for a moment, then begins typing.

15. INT: DAY. PAUL'S APARTMENT

Several hours later. With the sounds of PAUL'S typing continuing to come from the workroom, we see RASHID stand on a chair next to the bookcase in the larger room and deposit the brown paper bag behind the books on one of the upper shelves.

16. INT: NIGHT. PAUL'S APARTMENT

A shot of RASHID asleep in PAUL'S bed. Lying next to him on the bed is an open, half-read copy of one of PAUL'S books: The Mysterious Barricades, by Paul Benjamin.

Cut to a shot of PAUL sleeping on the floor of the workroom.

17. INT: DAY. PAUL'S APARTMENT

PAUL is in his workroom, sitting at his desk, typing. We see more index cards pinned to the wall. PAUL hears a loud crash from the other room. He pops up from his desk, exasperated, then walks to the door and opens it. Shot of the other room: RASHID is standing there, looking down at broken dishes.

PAUL
(Irritated) Jesus, do you make a lot of noise. Can't you see I'm trying to work?

RASHID
(Mortified) I'm sorry. They just . . . they just slipped out of my hands.

PAUL
A little less clumsiness around here would be nice, don't you think?

RASHID
(Growning defensive) I'm a teenager. All teenagers are clumsy. It's because we're still growing. We don't know where our bodies end and the world begins.

PAUL
The world is going to end pretty soon if you don't learn fast. *(Pause. PAUL reaches into his pocket and pulls out his wallet, then removes a twenty-dollar bill)* Look, why not make yourself useful? I'm just about out of smokes. Go around the corner to the Brooklyn Cigar Company and buy me two tins of Schimmelpenninck Medias. *(Hands the bill to RASHID)*

RASHID

(Taking the bill) Twenty dollars is a lot of money. Are you sure you can trust me with it? I mean, aren't you afraid I might steal it?

PAUL

If you want to steal it, that's your business. At least I won't have you around here making noise. *(Pause)* It might be worth it.

RASHID, *visibly hurt by* PAUL'S *remark, puts the money in his pocket. For once, he is unable to come up with a quick retort.*

RASHID *walks out of the apartment.* PAUL *watches the door slam. Slight pause, then he bends down and starts picking up the broken dishes.*

18. INT: DAY. PAUL'S APARTMENT

The workroom. A few minutes later. PAUL *returns to his desk and begins to type. Almost immediately, the ribbon jams. He lets out a groan, then opens the typewriter to inspect the damage.*

19. EXT: DAY. THE BROOKLYN CIGAR CO., AS SEEN FROM ACROSS THE STREET

Eight o'clock in the morning. We see AUGGIE *on the corner, getting ready to take his daily photograph. Cut to the corner as seen through the lens of the camera. Hustle and bustle, people on their way to work. Automobile traffic, buses, delivery trucks. We hear the shutter click. The picture freezes.*

20. INT: DAY. PAUL'S APARTMENT

The workroom. PAUL *is sitting at his desk, writing. A loud crash from the other room punctuates the silence. He jumps in his chair.*

PAUL

(Groans) Shit.

He stands up, goes to the door, opens it. Shot of RASHID *standing precari-
ously on the arm of a chair, his right hand groping behind the books on
the top shelf of the bookcase. Several books have already fallen to the
floor.*

PAUL (cont'd)

Jesus Christ. Are you at it again?

RASHID *turns at the sound of* PAUL'S *voice, momentarily losing his balance. As he grabs hold of the bookcase again to steady himself, more
books fall off the shelf and come tumbling to the floor. An instant later, he
lands on the floor as well.*

PAUL (cont'd)

What is it with you, anyway? You're like a human wrecking ball.

RASHID

(Climbing to his feet. Ashamed) I'm sorry. I'm really sorry . . . I was trying
to reach for one of the books up there . . . *(Points)* And then, I don't know,
the sky fell on top of me.

PAUL

(With growing irritation) It just won't do, will it? I go two and a half years

5 3

without being able to write a word, and then, when I finally get started on something, when it looks as though I might actually be coming to life again, you show up and start breaking everything in my house. It just won't do, will it?

RASHID

(Hurt, subdued) I didn't ask to come here. You invited me, remember? *(Pause)* If you want me to leave, all you have to do is say so.

PAUL

How long have you been here?

RASHID

Three nights.

PAUL

And how long did I tell you you could stay?

RASHID

Two or three nights.

PAUL

It sounds like our time is up, doesn't it?

RASHID

(Looking down at floor) I'm sorry I messed up. You've been very kind to
me . . . (Walks toward the bed, picks up the backpack from the floor,
and begins stuffing his things into it) But all good things have to come to
an end, right?

PAUL

No hard feelings, okay? It's a small place, and I can't get my work done
with you around.

RASHID

You don't have to apologize. (Pause) The coast is probably clear now
anyway.

PAUL

(Softening) Are you going to be all right?

RASHID

Absolutely. The world is my oyster. (Pause) Whatever that means. (He
looks up at the bookshelf, studying the spot where the bag is hidden. He
makes a quick, resolute decision to leave the bag where it is)

PAUL

Do you need some money? Some extra clothes?

RASHID

Not a penny, not a stitch. I'm cool, man. (Hoists the backpack over his
shoulder, begins walking toward the door)

PAUL

(A little stunned by RASHID'S decisiveness) Take good care of yourself,
okay?

RASHID

You too. And make sure the light is green before you cross the street. (*Reaches for the doorknob, opens the door, hesitates, turns around*) Oh, by the way, I liked your book. I think you're a hell of a good writer. (*Without waiting for a response, he opens the door again and leaves*)

Shot of PAUL *standing alone in the middle of the room. He walks to the window and looks outside. Shot of the street below. After three or four seconds,* RASHID *emerges from the building. Without glancing back, he begins walking down the street.*

Cut to PAUL *standing at the window. He lights up a cigar. Cut back to the street.* RASHID *has disappeared. An instant later, a blind man comes walking around the corner, tapping his white cane on the sidewalk.*

21. INT: NIGHT. AUGGIE'S APARTMENT

The windows are open and traffic noises can be heard from the street below.

AUGGIE *alone. Jazz is playing on his tape machine. He takes a TV dinner out of the oven, then sits down at the kitchen table and begins to eat. Fade out.*

The meal is over. AUGGIE *pours himself a shot of bourbon. He drinks it down in one swallow and smacks his lips, exhaling loudly. Stares blankly ahead of him for a moment. Then he reaches for a paperback copy of* Crime and Punishment *open on the table. As he finds his place in the book, he lights a cigarette. After one or two puffs, he begins to cough: a deep, rattling, prolonged smoker's cough. He pounds his chest. It doesn't help. He stands up, banging the table as the coughing fit continues. He begins to stagger around the kitchen, cursing between breaths. In his rage, he sweeps everything off the table: glass, bottle, book, remnants of the TV dinner. The cough subsides, then starts up again. He grabs hold of the kitchen sink and spits into the basin.*

22. INT: DAY. PAUL'S APARTMENT

The main room. We hear the sound of PAUL typing. A loud, insistent banging is heard at the front door. Cut to PAUL opening the door. RASHID'S AUNT EM is standing in the hall. She is a black woman of about forty, dressed in clothes that suggest she works in an office.

> AUNT EM
>
> *(Angrily)* Is your name Paul Benjamin?

> PAUL
>
> *(Taken aback)* What can I do for you?

> AUNT EM
>
> *(Barging into the apartment)* I just want to know what your game is, mister, that's all.

> PAUL
>
> *(Horrified. Watching her as she charges around the room)* How the hell did you get into the building?

> AUNT EM
>
> What do you mean, how'd I get in? I pushed the door and walked in. What do you think?

> PAUL
>
> *(Muttering to himself)* The damn lock's broken again. *(Pause, as he returns AUNT EM'S glare. Louder)* And so you just barge in on strangers, is that what you do? Is that *your* game?

> AUNT EM
>
> I'm looking for my nephew, Thomas.

> PAUL
>
> Thomas? Who's Thomas?

> AUNT EM
>
> Don't give me any of that. I know he's been here. You can't fool me, mister.

PAUL

I'm telling you, I don't know anyone named Thomas.

AUNT EM

Thomas Cole. Thomas Jefferson Cole. My nephew.

PAUL

You mean Rashid?

AUNT EM

Rashid? *Rashid!* Is that what he told you his name was?

PAUL

Well, whatever his name is, he's not here anymore. He left two days ago, and I haven't heard from him since.

AUNT EM

And what was he doing here in the first place? That's what I want to know. What's a man like you messing around with a black boy like Thomas for? Are you some kind of pervert, or what?

PAUL

(*Losing patience*) Look, lady, that's enough. If you don't calm down, I'm going to throw you out. Do you hear me? Right now!

AUNT EM

(*Getting a grip on herself*) I just want to know where he is.

PAUL

As far as I know, he went back to his parents.

AUNT EM

(*Incredulous*) His parents? Is that what he told you? His *parents?*

PAUL

That's what he said. He told me he lived with his mother and father on East Seventy-fourth Street.

AUNT EM

(*Defeated, shaking her head*) I always knew that boy had an imagination, but now he's gone and made up a whole new life for himself. *(Pause)* Do you mind if I sit down? *(PAUL gestures to a chair; she sits down)* He's been living with me and his uncle Henry since he was a baby. And we don't live in Manhattan. We live in Boerum Hill. In the projects.

PAUL

He doesn't go to the Trinity School?

AUNT EM

He goes to John Jay High School in Brooklyn.

PAUL

(Beginning to show concern) And his parents?

AUNT EM

His mother's dead, and he hasn't seen his father in twelve years.

PAUL

(Softly, almost to himself) I shouldn't have let him go.

AUNT EM

(Studying PAUL) Which brings me back to my original question. What was he doing here in the first place?

PAUL

I was about to get run over by a car, and your nephew pulled me back. He saved my life. *(Pause)* I sensed he was in trouble, so I offered to put him up for a few days. Maybe I should have pressed him a little more, I don't know. I feel pretty stupid about it now.

AUNT EM

He's in trouble, all right. But I don't have any idea what it is.

PAUL

(Sits down in a chair, lets out a sigh, thinks for a moment. Turns to AUNT EM) Do you want something to drink? A beer? A glass of water?

AUNT EM

(Primly) No thank you.

PAUL

(Lapses into thought again. After a moment) Has anything happened lately? Anything unusual or unexpected?

AUNT EM

(Thinks) Well, one thing I suppose, but I don't think it has anything to do with this. *(Pause)* A friend of mine called about two weeks ago and said she'd spotted Thomas's father working at some gas station outside of Peekskill.

PAUL

And you told your nephew about it?

AUNT EM

(Shrugs) I figured he had a right to know.

PAUL

And?

AUNT EM

And nothing. Thomas looked at me straight in the eye and said, "I don't have a father. As far as I'm concerned, that son-of-a-bitch is dead."

PAUL

Those are pretty hostile words.

The camera slowly closes in on her face as she speaks:

AUNT EM

His father walked out on his mother a couple of months after he was born. Louisa was Henry's younger sister, and she and the baby moved in with us. Four or five years go by, and then one day Cyrus shows up out of the blue, tail between his legs, wanting to patch things up with Louisa. I thought Henry was going to tear Cyrus apart when he saw him walk through the door. They're both big men, those two, and if they ever started to tangle, you'd see some teeth jumping on the floor, I guarantee it . . . So Cyrus persuaded Louisa to go out with him to talk things over in quiet. And the poor girl never came back.

PAUL (OFF)

You mean she just ran off with him and left her little boy behind?

AUNT EM

Don't put words in my mouth. What I'm saying is she drove off in Cyrus's car and went to the Five-Spot Lounge with him for a drink. What I'm saying is that he imbibed too much in the way of alcohol and that when they finished their little talk three hours later and got back in the car, he was in no shape to drive. But he drove the car anyway, and before he could get her back to where she lived, the damn fool ran a red light and went straight into a truck. Louisa got thrown through the windshield and was killed. Cyrus lived, but he came out of it a cripple. His left arm was so mangled, the doctors had to cut it off. Small punishment for what he did, if you ask me.

PAUL (OFF)

(Aghast) Jesus.

AUNT EM

Jesus had nothing to do with it. If He'd been involved, He would have seen to it that things worked out the opposite from what they did.

PAUL (OFF)

It can't have been easy on him. Walking around with that on his conscience all these years.

AUNT EM

No, I don't suppose it has. He was broken up like nobody's business in that hospital when he found out Louisa was dead.

PAUL (OFF)

And he's never tried to get in touch with his son?

AUNT EM

Henry told Cyrus he'd kill him if he ever showed his face around our house again. When Henry makes a threat like that, people tend to take him seriously.

PAUL and AUNT EM *look at each other. Cut to shot of the kitchen sink. Water is slowly dripping from the faucet. Hold for two or three beats.*

23. EXT: DAY. A COUNTRY ROAD OUTSIDE OF PEEKSKILL

Early morning. Trees, shrubs, twittering birds. We see RASHID trudging down the road. Dissolve to:

The same road, a mile on. RASHID looks up. Cut to:

24. EXT: DAY. COLE'S GARAGE

The garage is a ramshackle, two-story building. Over the main door is a clumsily executed hand-painted sign that reads: COLE'S GARAGE. *Two Chevron gas pumps stand alone in the front: weeds sprout through the macadam. To one side of the station is a grassy area with a weather-beaten picnic table.*

The double garage doors are open. We see a man in there working on the engine of an old Chevrolet. The hood is up, which obscures the man's face, but we can see that he is wearing mechanic's overalls and that the color of his skin is black.

He is a large, burly man of about forty. Once he appears from behind the hood, we see that his left hand is missing. A metal hook juts out of his sleeve.

This is RASHID'S father, CYRUS COLE.

25. EXT: DAY. THE SIDE OF THE COUNTRY ROAD, DIRECTLY OPPOSITE COLE'S GARAGE

We see RASHID sitting on the hood of a rusted car across the road from the garage. He is motionless, hugging his knees and gazing intently in the direction of the camera. Hold for three, four beats.

26. INT: DAY. COLE'S GARAGE

A bit later. CYRUS, still busily at work on the Chevrolet, glances up and sees RASHID across the road. He studies him for a moment, then returns to his work.

27. EXT: DAY. THE SIDE OF THE COUNTRY ROAD, DIRECTLY OPPOSITE COLE'S GARAGE

An hour later. We see RASHID sitting on the hood of the car, as before. This time he has his sketch pad propped against his knees and is doing a pencil drawing of the garage across the way.

28. EXT: DAY. OUTSIDE COLE'S GARAGE

An hour later. We see CYRUS emerge from the garage carrying a brown paper bag. He walks over to the picnic table, sits down, and takes out his lunch from the bag: a ham sandwich, an apple, a can of iced tea. As he chews and drinks, he studies RASHID across the road. Every now and then, a car or truck passes by.

The camera cuts between RASHID and CYRUS. RASHID, working busily on his drawing, pretends not to notice he is being watched.

At last, CYRUS finishes his lunch. He crumples up the paper bag, gets to his feet, and tosses his garbage into a rusted metal trash can next to the picnic table. Instead of going back to work, he crosses the road.

29. EXT: DAY. THE SIDE OF THE COUNTRY ROAD, DIRECTLY OPPOSITE COLE'S GARAGE

Master shot. As CYRUS approaches, RASHID looks up, meeting the man's eyes for the first time. Before CYRUS can get close enough to see the drawing, RASHID closes the sketch pad and presses it against his chest. He makes no attempt to stand up.

CYRUS

You going to sit here all day?

RASHID

I don't know. I haven't decided yet.

CYRUS

Why don't you pick some other spot? It gives a man the creeps to be
stared at all morning.

RASHID

It's a free country, isn't it? As long as I'm not trespassing on your property,
I can stay here till kingdom come.

CYRUS

(Approaching the car. RASHID jumps off the hood as CYRUS draws closer)
Let me give you some useful information, son. There's two dollars and
fifty-seven cents in that cash register over there (gestures with his hand to
the garage across the road), and considering all the time you've put in
casing the joint so far, you won't make but about fifty cents an hour for
all your pains. However you slice it, that's a losing proposition.

RASHID

I'm not going to rob you, mister. (Amused) Do I look like a thief?

CYRUS

I don't know what you look like, boy. As far as I can tell, you sprouted up
like a mushroom in this spot last night. (Pause. Studies RASHID more
closely) You live in this town—or on your way from here to there?

RASHID

Just passing through.

CYRUS

Just passing through. A lonesome traveller with a knapsack on his back
plops himself across from my garage to admire the view. There's other
places to roam, kid, that's all I'm saying. You don't want to make a
nuisance of yourself.

RASHID

I'm working on a sketch. That old garage of yours is so rundown, it's kind
of interesting.

CYRUS

It's rundown, all right. But drawing a picture won't improve the way it looks. *(Zeroing in on the sketch pad pressed against RASHID'S chest)* Let's see what you did, Rembrandt.

RASHID

(Thinking fast) It'll cost you five bucks.

CYRUS

Five bucks! You mean you're going to charge me five bucks just to look at it?

RASHID

Once you look at it, you're going to want to buy it from me. That's guaranteed. And that's the price: five bucks. So if you're not willing to spring for it, you might as well not bother to look. It'll just tear you up inside and make you miserable.

CYRUS

(Shaking his head) Son-of-a-bitch. You're some piece of work, aren't you?

RASHID

(Shrugs) I just tell it like it is, mister. *(Pause)* If I'm getting on your nerves, though, you might want to think about hiring me.

CYRUS

(Growing annoyed) Do you have eyes in your head, or are those brown things bulging out of your sockets just marbles? You've been sitting here all day, and how many cars have you seen drive up and ask for gas?

RASHID

Not a one.

CYRUS

Not a one. Not one customer all day. I bought this broken-down shit-hole of a place three weeks ago, and if business don't pick up soon, I'm going straight down the skids. What do I want to be hiring someone for? I can't even pay my own wages.

RASHID

It was just a thought.

CYRUS

Yeah, well, do your thinking somewhere else, Michelangelo. I got work to
do.

CYRUS *begins to leave. We see him crossing the road, shaking his head.*
Halfway there, he suddenly stops, turns, and shouts at RASHID:

CYRUS (cont'd)

Who do you think I am, the fucking State Employment Agency?

**30. EXT: DAY. THE SIDE OF THE COUNTRY ROAD, DIRECTLY OPPOSITE
COLE'S GARAGE**

Half an hour later. We see RASHID *sitting on the hood of the car, as before.*
This time he is eating a sandwich, chewing slowly as he gazes ahead.

31. INT: DAY. COLE'S GARAGE

We see CYRUS *at work on the Chevrolet. Every now and then, he glances*
up to look at RASHID.

CYRUS *finishes the job he has been doing. He slams the hood of the*
Chevrolet shut. Quick cut to:

**32. EXT: DAY. THE SIDE OF THE COUNTRY ROAD, DIRECTLY OPPOSITE
COLE'S GARAGE**

CYRUS *enters the frame and hoists himself onto the hood of the car—right*
next to RASHID. *A long silence.*

CYRUS

(Trying to be friendly) I'll tell you what. You want to work, I'll give you a
job. Nothing permanent, mind you, but that upstairs room over there
(turns, points)—the one above the office—is a hell of a mess. It looks like

they've been throwing junk in there for twenty years, and it's time it got cleaned up.

                              RASHID

(Playing it cool) What's your offer?

                              CYRUS

Five bucks an hour. That's the going rate, isn't it? *(Looks at his wristwatch)* It's a quarter past two now. My wife's picking me up at five-thirty, so that'll give you about three hours. If you can't finish today, you can do the rest tomorrow.

                              RASHID

(Getting to his feet) Is there a benefits package, or are you hiring me on a freelance basis?

                              CYRUS

Benefits?

                              RASHID

You know, health insurance, dental plan, paid vacation. It's not fun being exploited. Workers have to stand up for their rights.

                              CYRUS

I'm afraid we'll be working on a strictly freelance basis.

                              RASHID

(Long pause. Pretending to think it over) Five dollars an hour? *(Another pause)* I'll take it.

                              CYRUS

(Cracking a faint smile. Extends his right hand) The name is Cyrus Cole.

                              RASHID

I'm Paul. Paul Benjamin.

They shake hands.

33. INT: DAY. THE BROOKLYN CIGAR CO.

It is a slow hour in the middle of the afternoon. AUGGIE is sitting on a stool behind the counter, reading his paperback copy of Dostoyevsky's Crime and Punishment. *JIMMY ROSE is working in silence near the far wall on the other side of the counter, diligently and awkwardly straightening the stacks of newspapers and magazines.*

The bell on the front door rattles, signalling the arrival of a customer. Shot of JIMMY stopping his work to look up in the direction of the door. From JIMMY POV: a woman enters the store. She is RUBY McNUTT (AUGGIE'S old flame). Mid-forties, wearing a sleeveless summer dress, her face registering a tumult of anxiety, determination, and self-consciousness. She wears a black patch over her left eye.

Shot of JIMMY looking in wonder at the patch. Shot of RUBY looking in the direction of the counter. Shot of AUGGIE sitting behind the counter, still immersed in his book, not bothering to glance up. Close-up of RUBY'S face: she is looking at AUGGIE. Her lips are trembling. She is obviously moved, but she is too afraid to speak. With the camera fixed on RUBY'S face, we hear:

JIMMY (OFF)

(Hesitantly) Auggie. *(No response. Pause)* Auggie, I think there's a customer.

Close-up of AUGGIE glancing up from his book. We see his expression change from one of indifference to recognition and astonishment.

Close-up of RUBY looking at him. She smiles tentatively. As they talk, JIMMY studies them with rapt attention.

RUBY

Auggie?

Shot of AUGGIE'S face: he is still too amazed to speak.

RUBY (cont'd)

It's really you, Auggie, isn't it?

AUGGIE

(Finally) Christ, Ruby, it's been so long. I figured you were dead.

RUBY

Eighteen and a half years.

AUGGIE

Is that all? I thought it was about three hundred.

RUBY

(Shyly, hesitantly) You're looking good, Auggie.

AUGGIE

No I'm not. I look like shit. And so do you, Ruby. You look just awful.
(Pause, with increasing bitterness) What's with the patch, anyway?
What'd you do with that old blue marble—hock it for a bottle of gin?

RUBY

(Hurt, embarrassed) I don't want to talk about it. (Pause) If you really
want to know, I lost it. And I'm not sorry I did. That eye was cursed,
Auggie, and it never gave me nothing but grief.

AUGGIE

And you think it looks better to go around dressed up like Captain Hook?

RUBY

(In a low voice, trying to maintain her composure and dignity) You
always were a son-of-a-bitch, weren't you? A little weasel with a quick,
dirty mouth.

AUGGIE

At least I've stayed true to myself. Which is more than I can say about
some people.

RUBY

(Again, she tries to shrug it off. Takes a deep breath) I've got something to
talk to you about, and the least you can do is listen. You owe me that
much. I drove all the way from Pittsburgh to see you, and I'm not going
back until you've heard me out.

AUGGIE

Fine. Talk away, lady of my dreams. I'm all ears.

RUBY

(Glancing around the store. Sees JIMMY studying her) This is private,
Auggie. Just between you and I.

AUGGIE

(Addressing JIMMY with unaccustomed irritation) You heard her,
pipsqueak. The lady and I have private business to discuss. Go outside
and stand in front of the door. If anyone tries to come in, tell 'em we're
closed. You got that?

JIMMY

Sure, Auggie, I got it. *(Pause)* The store's closed. *(Pause, thinks)* And when
do I tell them it's open?

AUGGIE

(Snaps) When I tell you it's open. It's open when I tell you it's open!

JIMMY

(Hurt) Okay, Auggie, I got it. You don't have to yell.

JIMMY *goes outside and posts himself in front of the door.*

AUGGIE

(Looking closely at RUBY as he lights a cigarette) All right, sugar, what's on your mind?

RUBY

(Pause. Self-conscious) Don't look at me like that, Auggie. It gives me the creeps.

AUGGIE

Like what?

RUBY

Like what you're doing. I'm not going to eat you up. (Pause) I need your help, and if you keep staring at me like that, I might start screaming.

AUGGIE

(With an edge of sarcasm) Help, huh? And I don't suppose this help has anything to do with money, does it?

RUBY

Don't rush me, okay? You're jumping to conclusions before I've even said anything. (Pause) And besides, it's not for me. (Pause. Realizing she's let the cat out of the bag. In desperation, she plunges on) It's for our daughter.

AUGGIE

(Shocked, growing belligerent) Our daughter? Is that what you said? Our daughter? I mean, you might have a daughter, but I sure as hell don't. And even if I did—which I don't—she wouldn't be our daughter.

RUBY

Her name is Felicity, and she just turned eighteen. (Pause) She ran away from Pittsburgh last year, and now she's living in some shit-hole here in Brooklyn with a guy named Chico. Strung out on crack, four months pregnant. (Pause) I can't bear to think about that baby. Our grandchild, Auggie. Just think of it. Our grandchild.

AUGGIE

(Waving her off, impatient) Stop it, already. Just stop all this crap right now. (Pause. Changing the subject. With contempt) Was that your idea to call her Felicity?

RUBY

It means "happiness."

AUGGIE

I know what it means. That still don't make it a good name.

RUBY

I don't know who else to turn to, Auggie.

AUGGIE

You've suckered me before, darling, remember? Why should I believe
you now?

RUBY

Why would I lie to you, Auggie? You think it was easy to come here and
walk into this place? Why would I do it if I didn't have to?

AUGGIE

That's what you told me when I shoplifted that necklace for you. You
remember, baby, don't you? The judge gave me a choice: either go to
the can or enlist. So, instead of going to college, I wind up in the navy for
four years, I watch men lose their arms and legs, I nearly get my head
blown off, and you, sweet Ruby McNutt, you run off and marry that
asshole, Bill.

RUBY

You didn't write to me for more than a year. What was I supposed to
think?

AUGGIE

Yeah, well, I lost my pen. By the time I got a new one, I was clean out of
paper.

RUBY

It was over with Bill before you ever came home. Maybe you don't
remember it now, but you were pretty hot to see me back then.

AUGGIE

You weren't so lukewarm yourself. At least at first.

RUBY

It fizzled, baby. That's the way it goes. But we had our times, didn't we? It wasn't all bad.

AUGGIE

A couple of moments, I'll grant you that. A second or two snatched from the jaws of eternity.

RUBY

And that's how Felicity came into the picture. During one of those two seconds.

AUGGIE

You're conning me, sweetheart. I ain't responsible for no baby.

RUBY

Then why do you think I married Frank? I was already pregnant, and I didn't have much time. Say what you like, but at least he gave my kid a name.

AUGGIE

Good old Frank. And how is fat Mr. Grease Monkey these days?

RUBY

Who the hell knows? *(Shrugs)* He dropped out of sight fifteen years ago.

AUGGIE

Fifteen years ago? *(Shakes head)* It won't wash, pumpkin. No mother waits fifteen years to tell a man he's a father. I wasn't born yesterday, you know.

RUBY

(Her lips start to tremble. We see tears falling from her one good eye) I thought I could handle it. I didn't want to bug you. I thought I could handle it on my own, but I couldn't. She's in real bad, Auggie.

AUGGIE

Nice try, old girl. I'd like to help you out. You know, for old time's sake. But all my spare cash is tied up in a business venture, and I haven't collected my profits yet. Too bad. You caught me at the wrong time.

RUBY

(Still crying) You're a cold-hearted bastard, aren't you? How'd you ever get so mean, Auggie?

AUGGIE

I know you think I'm lying to you, but I'm not. Every word I told you is the God's honest truth.

Pause. Then cut to the store entrance. The door suddenly bursts open as an IRATE CUSTOMER pushes his way past JIMMY. We see JIMMY futilely trying to hold him back.

AUGGIE (cont'd)

(Shouting at customer. Beside himself) The store's closed! Didn't you hear what the kid told you? The goddamn store is closed!

34. INT: DAY. THE UPSTAIRS ROOM OF COLE'S GARAGE

We see RASHID working diligently. The place is a pigsty, cluttered with all sorts of debris: rusty bicycles, rags, automotive parts, a female mannequin, broken radios, shower curtains, etc. One by one, RASHID drags or carries these things toward the door. At one point, he finds a small, portable black-and-white TV hidden under a rug. The rabbit ears are broken, the casing is covered with dust, but other than that it seems to be in reasonably good shape.

35. EXT: DAY. OUTSIDE COLE'S GARAGE

RASHID and CYRUS are carrying the debris from the upstairs room and throwing it into the back of an old red pickup truck. Once they get rid of a load, they go back inside for more. Since RASHID is faster, they are working out of phase: when one is outside, the other is inside.

They work in silence. CYRUS begins to huff and puff from going up and down the stairs. Eventually, after a number of trips, he drops a load into the truck and stops. He leans against the truck, pulls out a large, cheap, half-smoked cigar from his shirt pocket, and lights up. *Close-up of the hook as he strikes the match. After one or two puffs on the cigar, RASHID appears with another load and tosses it into the truck.*

CYRUS

Time for a pause.

Without further ado, RASHID promptly sits down on the rear bumper of the truck. He does it so quickly, the effect is comical. He watches CYRUS smoke. Two or three beats.

RASHID

I don't mean to be nosey, but I was wondering what happened to your arm.

CYRUS

(Holds up his hook and studies it for a moment) An ugly piece of hardware, isn't it? *(Pause)* I'll tell you what happened to my arm. *(Pause. Remembering)* I'll tell you what happened. *(Pause)* Twelve years ago, God looked down on me and said, "Cyrus, you're a bad, stupid, selfish man. First of all, I'm going to fill your body with spirits, and then I'm going to put you behind the wheel of a car, and then I'm going to make you crash that car and kill the woman who loves you. But you, Cyrus, I'm going to let you live, because living is a lot worse than death. And just so you don't forget what you did to that poor girl, I'm going to rip off your arm and replace it with a hook. If I wanted to, I could rip off both your arms and both your legs, but I'm going to be merciful and just take off your left arm. Every time you look at your hook, I want you to remember what a bad, stupid, selfish man you are. Let that be a lesson to you, Cyrus, a warning to mend your ways."

RASHID

(Impressed by the sincerity of CYRUS'S speech) And have you mended them?

CYRUS

I don't know. I try. Every day I keep on trying, but it's no easy task for a man to change his nature. *(Pause)* I'm off the booze, though. Haven't had a drop in six years. And now I've got me a wife. Doreen. Best damned woman I've ever known. *(Pause)* And a little boy, too. Cyrus Junior.

(*Pause*) So things have definitely improved since I got fitted with this hook. If I can just turn this goddamn garage around, I'll be in pretty good shape.

                        RASHID
You named the kid after yourself, huh?

                        CYRUS
(*Smiling at the thought of his son*) That boy's one in a million. A real tiger.

Cut to close-up of RASHID'S face. He seems to be growing more and more upset.

                    CYRUS (cont'd)
And what about you, kid? What's your story?

                        RASHID
(*Turning away*) Who, me? I don't have a story. I'm just a kid.

Fade out.

36. EXT: DAY. OUTSIDE COLE'S GARAGE

Late afternoon. RASHID and CYRUS continue loading debris into the back of the truck. We see the black-and-white portable TV sitting on the ground outside the office.

After a few moments, a ten-year-old blue Ford pulls up next to the truck and stops. It is driven by CYRUS'S wife, DOREEN. She is an attractive, self-possessed woman in her late twenties. CYRUS JUNIOR is sitting in a child-restraint seat in the back. He is two years old.

CYRUS'S face lights up when he sees the car. DOREEN cuts off the engine and gets out, smiling at her husband. RASHID, suddenly forgotten by CYRUS, watches the exchange with keen interest.

CYRUS

Hi, baby. How'd it go today?

DOREEN

(Joking) If I have to wash one more old lady's hair, I think my fingers would fall off. *(She kisses him on the cheek)*

CYRUS

Busy, huh? That's good, because things around here sure were sleepy today.

DOREEN

(Opening the back of the car, unstrapping JUNIOR from his seat, and picking him up in her arms) Don't worry, Cy. It's early days yet. *(Addressing JUNIOR, but at the same time catching sight of RASHID)* Say hello to Daddy.

JUNIOR

(Squirming in his mother's arms, excited at seeing his father) Dada! Dada!

CYRUS

(Taking the boy in his arms and giving him a big kiss) Hey there, little tiger. And what did you do today?

DOREEN

(Addressing RASHID as she hands the baby to CYRUS) Hello.

                              RASHID

(Shyly) Hello.

                              CYRUS

(Noticing the exchange between DOREEN and RASHID) Jesus, I almost
forgot you were here. Doreen, this is Paul. My new assistant.

DOREEN extends her right hand to RASHID.

                              RASHID

(Shaking DOREEN'S hand) It's only temporary. On a freelance basis.

                              CYRUS

(Turning JUNIOR toward RASHID) And this one, in case you haven't
guessed, is Junior.

                              RASHID

(Studying JUNIOR carefully. Mumbles in a barely audible voice) Hi there,
little brother.

                              CYRUS

(To JUNIOR) Say hi to Paul.

                              JUNIOR

Hi there, little brother.

                              CYRUS

(To DOREEN) He's helping me clean out that upstairs room. Might as well
get this place looking good, anyway. (To RASHID) I guess that's it for
today, sport. Come back tomorrow morning at eight, and you can pick
up where you left off. (Starts walking to the office with JUNIOR in his
arms)

We see him through the window: opening the cash register, pocketing the
money, turning out the lights, then coming out and closing the garage
doors. In the foreground, we see RASHID standing with DOREEN. He looks
down at the ground, too shy to say a word to her. She studies him with a
mixture of curiosity and amusement. When CYRUS is finished closing up,
he walks toward them and says to RASHID:

Do you want me to pay you now, or can you wait until tomorrow?

RASHID

Tomorrow's fine. There's no rush.

37. EXT: EARLY EVENING. OUTSIDE COLE'S GARAGE

A little later. We see RASHID *sitting next to the TV outside the office door. He is utterly still. Hold for two, three beats.*

38. INT: EARLY EVENING. INSIDE THE OFFICE OF COLE'S GARAGE

We see a pencil drawing being slid under the door. It is an excellent rendering of the garage as seen from across the road.

The camera moves in on the drawing until it occupies the entire screen. Hold for two, three beats.

Fade out.

39. INT: DAY. PAUL'S APARTMENT

PAUL *opens the door.* RASHID *is standing in the hall, holding the black-and-white TV in his arms. The knapsack is on his back. His clothes have become a little shabbier since the last time we saw him.*

PAUL

(Surprised) Hey, it's you.

RASHID

(Serious) I wanted to give you this as a token of my appreciation.

PAUL

Appreciation for what?

RASHID

I don't know. For helping me out.

PAUL

(Eyeing TV suspiciously) Where did you get that thing?

RASHID

I bought it. Twenty-nine ninety-five on sale at Goldbaum's TV and Radio. (Hands TV to PAUL, who takes it in his arms. RASHID smiles) Well, that just about takes care of it, I guess. You'll be able to watch the ball games now. You know, as a little break from your work. (Begins to leave)

PAUL

Where the hell do you think you're going?

RASHID

Business appointment. I'm seeing my broker at three o'clock.

PAUL

Cut it out, will you? Just cut it out and come back here.

RASHID

(Looking at his watch. Shrugs) I don't have much time. (Returns to the doorway, enters the apartment)

PAUL

(Puts TV on the stereo cabinet) Close the door. (RASHID closes the door) Sit down in that chair. (Points. RASHID sits down in the chair) Now listen carefully. Your aunt Em came here a couple of days ago. She was sick with worry, out of her mind. We had an interesting talk about you, Thomas. Do you understand what I'm saying? Your aunt thinks you're in trouble and so do I. Tell me about it, kid. I want to hear all about it right now.

RASHID realizes he is trapped. Shrugs. Smiles weakly. Looks down at floor to avoid PAUL'S gaze. When he dares to look up again, PAUL is still glowering at him.

RASHID

You don't really want to know.

PAUL

(Impatient) I don't, huh? And what makes you such an authority on what I want or don't want?

RASHID

(Sighs, defeated) Okay, okay. (Pause) It's all so stupid. (Pause) There's this guy, see. Charles Clemm. The Creeper, that's what people call him. The kind of guy you don't want to cross paths with.

PAUL

And?

RASHID

(Hesitates) I crossed paths with him. That's why I'm trying to stay clear of my neighborhood. To make sure I don't run into him again.

PAUL

So that's the something you weren't supposed to see, huh?

Close-up of RASHID, becoming more animated as he talks.

RASHID

I just happened to be walking by. . . . All of a sudden, the Creeper and
this other guy come running out of this check-cashing place with masks
on their faces and guns in their hands. . . . They just about ran smack into
me. The Creeper recognized me, and I knew he knew I recognized him.
. . . If the guy from the check-cashing place hadn't rushed out then
screaming bloody murder, he would have shot me. I'm telling you, the
Creeper would have shot me right there on the sidewalk. But the noise
distracted him, and when he turned around to see what was happening,
I took off. . . . One more second, and I would have been dead.

PAUL

Why don't you go to the police?

RASHID

You're joking, right? I mean, that's your way of trying to be funny, right?

PAUL

If they put this Creeper in jail, then you'd be safe.

RASHID

The man has friends. And they're not likely to forgive me if I testify
against him.

PAUL

(Thinking) What makes you think you'll be any safer around here? It's
only about a mile away from where you live.

RASHID

It might not be far, but it's another galaxy. Black is black and white is
white, and never the twain shall meet.

PAUL

It looks like they've met in this apartment.

RASHID

That's because we don't belong anywhere. You don't fit into your world,
and I don't fit into mine. We're the outcasts of the universe.

PAUL

(Studying RASHID) Maybe. Or maybe it's the other people who don't
belong.

RASHID

Let's not get too idealistic.

PAUL

(Pause. Breaks into a smile) Fair enough. We wouldn't want to get carried away, would we? *(Pause)* Now call your aunt Em and let her know you're alive.

40. INT: EVENING. PAUL'S APARTMENT

PAUL *and* RASHID *are watching the Mets on television. They are both smoking little cigars. PAUL puffs on his calmly; RASHID coughs after each puff of his. He is clearly not used to smoking. The television has a defective tube: the reception is poor, and every now and then one of them stands up and bangs the top of the set to bring the picture back into focus. They watch the ball game in silence. Close-up of the TV screen: the batter swings. An announcer's voice is heard describing the action.*

41. EXT: LATE AFTERNOON. THE CORNER IN FRONT OF THE BROOKLYN CIGAR CO.

AUGGIE *is alone, closing up shop, looking particularly scruffy and unshaven. Just as he finishes pulling down the last metal gate, a car with Pennsylvania license plates comes speeding down Seventh Avenue and brakes to a sudden stop in front of the store. It is a ten-year-old Pontiac in rather sorry shape: belching smoke, with a defective muffler and a dented body. AUGGIE, distracted by the commotion, turns and looks at the car.*

From AUGGIE'S POV: we look into the car and see that the driver is RUBY McNUTT. leans out the open window and addresses AUGGIE in an urgent voice.

RUBY

Get in, Auggie. I've got something to show you.

AUGGIE

(Reluctant) You don't give up, do you?

RUBY

Just get in and shut up. I'm not asking you to do anything. I just need
you to come with me.

AUGGIE

Where to?

RUBY

(Impatient) Dammit, Auggie, don't ask so many questions. Just get in the
car.

AUGGIE shrugs. RUBY opens the right front door of the car, and he climbs
in. They drive off.

42. EXT: EVENING. THE STREETS OF BROOKLYN

We see RUBY'S car as it travels through the Brooklyn evening, making its
way down Seventh Avenue to Flatbush Avenue, then turning onto
Eastern Parkway and gliding past the Public Library and the Brooklyn
Museum as it penetrates the slums of Crown Heights and East New York.

RUBY

I told her she was going to meet her father.

AUGGIE

You what?

RUBY

It was the only way, Auggie. Otherwise, she wasn't going to let me see
her.

AUGGIE

I think you'd better stop the car and let me out.

RUBY

Relax, okay? You don't have to do anything. Just go in there and
pretend. It won't kill you to do a little favor like that. Besides, you might
even learn something.

AUGGIE

Yeah, like what?

RUBY

That I wasn't bullshitting you, sweetheart. At least you'll know I've been telling the truth.

AUGGIE

Look, I'm not saying you don't have a daughter. It's just that she's not my daughter.

RUBY

Wait till you see her, Auggie.

AUGGIE

And what's that supposed to mean?

RUBY

She looks just like you.

AUGGIE

(Irritated) Cut it out. Just cut it out, okay? It's starting to get on my nerves.

RUBY

When I told her I was going to bring her father, she kind of melted. It's the first time Felicity's talked nice to me since she left home. She's dying to meet you, Auggie.

They drive on in silence for a few more seconds. By now they have entered one of the worst, most dangerous parts of the city. We see broken-down, boarded-up buildings, vacant lots strewn with rubble, trash scattered on the sidewalks. RUBY turns down one of these streets, then brings the car to a halt in front of a walk-up building with spray-painted graffiti on the outer door: KILL THE COPS. AUGGIE and RUBY get out of the car and start walking toward the building. Down the street, in the distance, we see a black man pick up a metal garbage can and throw it violently to the ground. It lands with a loud crash.

AUGGIE

Nice neighborhood you've brought me to. Full of happy, prosperous people.

43. INT: EVENING. FELICITY'S APARTMENT

Close-up of a scarred green door. A knocking is heard from the other side. Pause. The knocking is heard again. After another pause, we hear feet padding toward the door. A second later a shoulder enters the frame. This is FELICITY from behind. She is dressed in a cheap flowered robe.

> FELICITY

Yeah? Who is it?

> RUBY (OFF)

It's me, honey. It's Mom.

We see FELICITY'S hand reach out and unbolt the lock. The door opens to reveal AUGGIE and RUBY standing in the hall. They both look nervous: RUBY expectant and hopeful, with a forced smile on her face, AUGGIE guarded and closed in on himself. Cut to a close-up of FELICITY'S face. She is a very pretty blonde of eighteen. Her expression is hostile, however, and there is a wasted look in her eyes. We see clumsily applied rouge on her cheeks, a slash of red lipstick on her lips. She runs her hand through her stringy, unwashed hair. Cut to a close-up of AUGGIE'S face. It is impossible to know what he is thinking.

As AUGGIE and RUBY enter the apartment, the camera backs up to show the room. It is a tawdry place with little furniture: a double mattress on the floor (the bed is unmade), a rickety wooden table and two chairs along the far wall (we see a box of Sugar Pops on the table), a hot plate, and an enormous color television near the mattress. The television is on, but the sound is off. Images of commercials flicker in the background during the rest of the scene. The only decoration is a large black-and-white poster of Jim Morrison Scotch-taped to one of the walls. Clothes are strewn everywhere: on the floor, on the table, on top of the television set.

By the time RUBY has shut the door behind her, FELICITY has already retreated to the other side of the room and is lighting a cigarette from a pack of Newports on the table. No one says anything. An awkward silence as FELICITY glares at her mother and AUGGIE.

> RUBY

(Finally) Well?

FELICITY

Well what?

RUBY

Aren't you going to say anything?

FELICITY

What do you want me to say?

RUBY

I don't know. Hello, Mom. Hello, Dad. Something like that.

FELICITY

(Takes a drag on her cigarette, looking AUGGIE up and down. Then, turning to RUBY) I don't got no daddy, you dig? I got born last week when some dog fucked you up the ass.

AUGGIE

(Muttering under his breath) Jesus Christ. This is all I need.

RUBY

(Trying to ignore the viciousness of her daughter's remark) You told me you wanted to meet him. Well, here he is.

FELICITY

Yeah, I might have said that. Chico told me to see what he was like, maybe there'd be some dough in it for us. Well, now I've seen him, and I can't say I'm too impressed. (*Pause. Turning to* AUGGIE) Hey, mister. Are you rich or what?

AUGGIE

(*Disgusted*) Yeah, I'm a millionaire. I walk around in disguise because I'm ashamed of all my money.

RUBY

(*To* FELICITY. *Imploringly*) Be nice, sweetie. We're just here to help you.

FELICITY

(*Snaps back*) Help? What the fuck do I need your help for? I've got a man, don't I? That's more than you can say for yourself, Hawkeye.

AUGGIE

Hey, hey, don't talk to your mother like that.

FELICITY

(*Crushing out her cigarette on the table. Ignoring* AUGGIE'S *remark. To*

her mother) You're telling me you actually went to bed with this guy? You're telling me you actually let him fuck you?

RUBY

(Mortified, struggling not to lose her composure) You can do whatever you want with your own life. We're thinking of the baby, that's all. We want you to get yourself cleaned up for the baby. Before it's too late.

FELICITY

Baby? And what baby is that?

RUBY

Your baby. The baby you're carrying around inside you.

FELICITY

Yeah, well, there ain't no baby in there now. You dig? There's nothing in there now.

RUBY

What are you talking about?

FELICITY

An abortion, stupid. *(Laughs bitterly)* I had an abortion the day before yesterday. So you don't have to bug me about that shit anymore. *(Laughs again. Defiantly, almost to herself)* Bye-bye, baby!

AUGGIE

(Taking hold of RUBY'S arm. RUBY is about to break into tears) Come on, let's get out of here. I've had enough.

RUBY *shrugs off* AUGGIE'S *hand and goes on looking at her daughter. As* FELICITY *speaks, the camera closes in on her face.*

FELICITY

Yeah, that's right, you better go. Chico'll be back any minute, and I'm sure your boyfriend doesn't want to mess with him. Chico's a real man. Not some scuzzy dickhead you find in last month's garbage. Do you hear what I'm saying? He'll chop up Mr. Dad here into little pieces. That's a promise. He'll kick the living shit out of him.

44. INT: DAY. PAUL'S APARTMENT

It is morning. RASHID is preparing a pot of coffee in the kitchenette. PAUL stumbles out of the bathroom, wiping his face with a towel. He has just woken up and is still groggy. He approaches the table.

PAUL

Ah, coffee. Smells good.

RASHID

(Handing him a cup) One sip of this stuff and your eyes will blast open.

PAUL

(Taking the cup and sitting down) Thanks. *(Begins to drink)*

RASHID

What time did you get to bed last night?

PAUL

I don't know. Two or three. It was pretty late.

RASHID

You work too hard, you know that?

PAUL

Once a story gets hold of you, it's hard to let go. *(Pause)* Besides, I'm making up for lost time.

RASHID

Just so you don't overdo it. You don't want to die of sleep deprivation before you finish.

PAUL

(Almost to himself. Looking up at the photo of Ellen on the wall) If you don't sleep, you don't dream. If you don't dream, you don't have nightmares.

RASHID

That's logical. And if you don't sleep, you don't need a bed. Saves you money, too. *(Pause)* So what's this story you're working on, anyway?

PAUL

If I tell you, I might not be able to finish it.

RASHID

Come on, just a little hint.

PAUL

(Smiling at RASHID'S eagerness. Pause) Okay, just a little hint. I can't tell you the story, but I'll tell you what gave me the idea for it.

RASHID

The inspiration.

PAUL

Yeah, right. The inspiration. It's a true story anyway, so I don't suppose it can hurt, can it?

RASHID

No way.

PAUL

All right. Listen carefully. (The camera slowly moves in for a close-up of

PAUL'S *face*) About twenty-five years ago, a young man went skiing alone in the Alps. There was an avalanche, the snow swallowed him up, and his body was never recovered.

RASHID (OFF)

(Mockingly) The end.

PAUL

No, not the end. The beginning. *(Pause)* His son was just a little boy at the time, but the years passed, and when he grew up, he became a skier, too. One day last winter, he went out by himself for a run down the mountain. He gets halfway to the bottom and then stops to eat his lunch next to a big rock. Just as he's unwrapping his cheese sandwich, he looks down and sees a body frozen in the ice—right there at his feet. He bends down to take a closer look, and suddenly he feels that he's looking into a mirror, that he's looking at himself. There he is—dead—and the body is perfectly intact, sealed away in a block of ice—like someone preserved in suspended animation. He gets down on all fours, looks right into the dead man's face, and realizes that he's looking at his father.

Cut to RASHID'S *face. We see him listening intently*

PAUL (cont'd) (OFF)

And the strange thing is that the father is younger than the son is now. The boy has become a man, and it turns out that he's older than his own father.

The camera holds on RASHID'S *face. After a moment:*

PAUL (OFF)

So what are you going to do today?

RASHID

(Shrugs) Read, think, do some drawings if I get in the mood.

He points to the coffee table: we see the sketch pad and a paperback copy of Shakespeare's Othello.

RASHID (cont'd)

But tonight I'm going to celebrate. That's definite.

PAUL

Celebrate? What for?

RASHID

It's my birthday. I'm seventeen years old (looks at wristwatch) as of forty-seven minutes ago, and I think I should celebrate having made it this far.

PAUL

(Raising coffee cup) Hey, hey. Happy birthday. Why didn't you tell me?

RASHID

(Deadpan) I just did.

PAUL

I mean earlier. We could have planned something.

Close-up of RASHID'S face.

RASHID

I don't like plans. I prefer to take things as they come.

45. INT: LATE AFTERNOON. THE BOOKSTORE

A small, cluttered independent bookshop.

The scene begins with a close-up of the clerk's face: APRIL LEE, a Eurasian woman in her mid- to late twenties. She is sitting behind the front counter with an open book before her. Her expression is puzzled, searching, as if she has just remembered or recognized something, but can't quite figure out what it is. We see her looking toward the back of the store, straining to listen in on PAUL and RASHID'S conversation.

RASHID (OFF)

Here we are. (Pause) Rembrandt's drawings. Edward Hopper. Van Gogh's letters.

PAUL (OFF)

Pick two or three. Now that the coffers are open, you might as well take advantage of me.

As PAUL *and* RASHID *start walking back in the direction of the counter,* APRIL *lowers her gaze and pretends to be reading. We see* PAUL *and* RASHID *enter the field of the camera from behind.* PAUL *puts a small pile of art books on the counter.*

PAUL

We'll take these, please.

APRIL *looks up; her eyes meet* PAUL'S. *They study each other for a brief moment—a significant exchange that does not escape* RASHID'S *notice.*

APRIL

Will that be cash or charge?

PAUL

(Taking out his wallet and looking inside) Better make it charge. *(Removes the credit card and hands it to* APRIL*)*

APRIL

(Looking at the card, smiles) I thought I recognized you. You're Paul Benjamin the writer, aren't you?

PAUL

(Both pleased and surprised) I confess.

APRIL

I keep waiting for the next novel to come out. Anything in the works?

PAUL

I, uh . . .

RASHID

(Butting in, with enthusiasm) It's coming along. At the rate he's going, he'll have a story finished by the end of the summer.

APRIL

Wonderful. When your next book is published, maybe you could come into the store and do a signing. I'm sure we could get a lot of people to show up.

PAUL

(Still staring at APRIL) Uh, actually, I tend to shy away from that kind of thing.

RASHID

(To APRIL) Excuse me for asking, but you aren't married, are you?

APRIL

(Taken aback) What!

RASHID

Perhaps I should rephrase the question. What I mean to say is, are you married or seriously involved with a significant other?

APRIL

(Still astonished. Bursts out laughing) No! At least I don't think I am!

RASHID

(Smiling with satisfaction) Good. Then may I have the honor of extending an invitation to you?

APRIL

An invitation?

Close-up of PAUL, listening to the exchange between RASHID and APRIL.

RASHID

Yes, an invitation. I apologize for springing it on you at the last minute, but Mr. Benjamin and I are attending a celebration tonight, and we would be most pleased if you chose to accompany us. *(Looking at PAUL)* Isn't that right, Mr. Benjamin?

PAUL

(Breaking into a broad smile) Absolutely. We would be honored.

APRIL

(Smiling) And what's the occasion of this celebration?

RASHID

It's my birthday.

APRIL

And how many people will be attending this birthday party?

RASHID

I wouldn't actually call it a party. It's more along the lines of a dinner in celebration of my birthday. *(Pause)* The guest list is quite restricted. So far, there's Mr. Benjamin and myself. If you accept, that would make three of us.

APRIL

(Ironic. With a crafty smile) Ah-hah, I see. A cozy dinner. But aren't threesomes a little awkward? How does the phrase go—

RASHID

Three's a crowd. Yes, I'm aware of that. But I have to keep an eye on Mr. Benjamin wherever he goes. To make sure he doesn't get himself into trouble.

APRIL

And what are you, his chaperone?

RASHID

(With a straight face) Actually, I'm his father.

APRIL *bursts out laughing, amused by the mounting silliness of the conversation.*

PAUL

It's true. Most people assume I'm *his* father. It's a logical assumption— given that I'm older than he is and so on. But the fact is, it's the other way around. He's my father, and I'm his son.

Close-up of APRIL'S face. She is still laughing.

Cut to:

46. INT: EVENING. CHINESE RESTAURANT IN BROOKLYN

In the background, we see a number of other customers. At one table, a Chinese family is celebrating a birthday. Toward the end of the scene, they all get up to pose for a group photograph. PAUL, RASHID, and APRIL are sitting together at a round table. They are in the middle of their meal.

PAUL

So your mother grew up in Shanghai?

APRIL

Until she was twelve. She moved here in 'forty-nine.

PAUL

And your father? Is he from New York?

APRIL

(Smiling) Muncie, Indiana. He and my mother met as students. But I'm from Brooklyn. My sisters and I were all born and bred right here.

PAUL

Just like me.

RASHID

Like me, too.

APRIL

I once read somewhere that one quarter of all the people in the United States have at least one relative who has lived in Brooklyn at one time or another.

RASHID

No wonder it's such a screwed-up place.

PAUL

(To APRIL) And the bookstore? Have you been working there long?

APRIL

It's just a summer job. Something to help pay the bills while I finish my dissertation.

PAUL

Your dissertation? What subject do you study?

APRIL

American literature. What else?

PAUL

What else. Of course, what else? And what are you writing about for
your thesis?

APRIL

(With mock pomposity) Visions of Utopia in Nineteenth-Century
American Fiction.

PAUL

Wow. You don't fool around, do you?

APRIL

(Smiling) Of course I fool around. But not so much when it comes to my
work, it's true. *(Pause)* Have you ever read *Pierre, or the Ambiguities*?

PAUL

Melville, huh? *(Smiles)* It's been a while.

APRIL

That's the subject of my last chapter.

PAUL

Not an easy book.

APRIL

Which explains why this hasn't been the easiest summer of my life.

RASHID

All the more reason to let 'er rip tonight, sweetheart. *(Raises glass)* You
know, go for the gusto.

APRIL *clinks her glass with* RASHID *and laughs merrily as* PAUL *looks on
and smiles. Cut to:*

47. INT: NIGHT. A BAR IN BROOKLYN

A noisy, crowded blue-collar hangout. APRIL, PAUL, and RASHID are standing together, looking rather tipsy. They are engaged in an animated three-way conversation, but we can't hear their voices over the din.

A song is playing on the jukebox ("Downtown Train," by Tom Waits). APRIL asks PAUL to dance. He agrees. As they dance, RASHID looks on. Even though the rhythm of the song is fast, PAUL and APRIL dance slowly, tentatively, not quite sure how to behave with each other.

After a moment, AUGGIE emerges from the back room with VIOLET, his flashy girlfriend, hanging on his arm. They are both plastered.

AUGGIE

(Drunk, smiling) Hey, man, good to see you.

PAUL

This is April Lee, Auggie. April, say hello to Auggie Wren.

APRIL

(Smiling) Hello, Auggie Wren.

AUGGIE

(Affecting the voice of a cowboy, tipping an imaginary hat) Howdy, Miss April, I'm right pleased to make your acquaintance. *(Turning to VIOLET)* And this pretty little lady here is Miss Vi-o-let Sanchez de Jalapeño, the hottest chili pepper this side of the Rio Grande. Ain't that so, baby?

VIOLET

Ees so, Auggie. And you not so cold, neither. Eh, baby?

PAUL, APRIL, *and* RASHID *nod hello to* VIOLET.

AUGGIE

So, what brings you to a dive like this?

PAUL

(Gesturing with thumb to RASHID; addressing AUGGIE) It's his birthday today, so we decided to whoop it up a little.

AUGGIE

(To RASHID*)* How old, kid?

RASHID

Seventeen.

AUGGIE

Seventeen? I remember when I was seventeen. Christ, I was one little whacked-out son-of-a-bitch when I was seventeen. Is that what you are, son? One little whacked-out crazy fella?

RASHID

(With feigned seriousness, nodding) Definitely. I'd say you've hit the nail on the head.

AUGGIE

Good. Keep it up, and maybe one day you'll grow up and become a great man like me. *(Bursts out laughing)*

PAUL *puts his arm around* AUGGIE, *addressing him in quieter tones. As they talk,* APRIL *and* VIOLET *look each other up and down, smiling awkwardly.* RASHID *strains to hear what* PAUL *and* AUGGIE *are saying to each other.*

                              PAUL

Hey, Auggie, I've just been thinking. You wouldn't need some help
around the store, would you? Some summer help while Vinnie's gone?

                             AUGGIE

(Thinking) Help? Hmm. It's possible. What did you have in mind?

                              PAUL

I'm thinking about the kid. I'm sure he'd do a good job for you.

                             AUGGIE

(Looking up and studying RASHID) Hey, kid. You interested in a job? I just
got word from your employment agency that you're looking for a position
in retail sales.

                             RASHID

A job? (Pause. Looks at PAUL) I definitely wouldn't turn down a job.

                             AUGGIE

Come around to the cigar store tomorrow morning at ten o'clock and
we'll talk about it, okay? We'll see what we can work out.

                             RASHID

Ten o'clock tomorrow morning. I'll be there.

                              PAUL

(Patting AUGGIE on the back) I owe you one. Don't forget.

48. INT: DAY. PAUL'S APARTMENT

Morning. PAUL and RASHID sitting at the table, eating breakfast. RASHID
is wearing a red T-shirt with the word "FIRE" emblazoned on the back in
white letters. We catch them in mid-conversation.

                              PAUL

It's 1942, right? And he's caught in Leningrad during the siege. I'm
talking about one of the worst moments in human history. Five hundred
thousand people died in that one place, and there's Bakhtin, holed up in
an apartment, expecting to be killed any day. He has plenty of tobacco,

but no paper to roll it in. So he takes the pages of a manuscript he's been working on for ten years and tears them up to roll his cigarettes.

                              RASHID

(Incredulous) His only copy?

                              PAUL

His only copy. *(Pause)* I mean, if you think you're going to die, what's more important, a good book or a good smoke? And so he huffed and he puffed, and little by little he smoked his book.

                              RASHID

(Thinks, then smiles) Nice try. You had me going for a second, but no . . . no writer would ever do a thing like that. *(Slight pause. Looking at PAUL)* Would he?

                              PAUL

(Amused) You don't believe me, huh? *(Stands up from the table and begins walking to the bookcase)* Look, I'll show you. It's all in this book.

PAUL *stands on a chair and reaches for a book on the top shelf. In doing so, he catches sight of the paper bag RASHID planted there in Scene 15. He studies it in bewilderment, then picks it up and dangles it in the air as he turns toward RASHID.*

                         PAUL (cont'd)

What's this?

                              RASHID

(Squirming with embarrassment) I don't know.

                              PAUL

Is it yours?

                              RASHID

Yeah, it might be.

                              PAUL

(Shrugs, not wanting to make an issue of it) Here, catch.

PAUL *tosses the bag in* RASHID's *direction. The bag breaks open in midair, and a shower of twenty-, fifty-, and hundred-dollar bills rains down from the ceiling.* PAUL *is stunned;* RASHID *is watching the world crumble before his eyes.*

Fade out.

49. INT: DAY. PAUL'S APARTMENT (LATER)

Fade in. A few minutes later. PAUL *and* RASHID *are sitting at the table again, the money stacked in neat piles between them. Again, we catch them in mid-conversation.*

PAUL
So you're saying it wasn't like that at all.

RASHID
Not exactly. I mean, there was more to it than I told you.

PAUL
Christ. You didn't just see what happened. They dropped the package on the ground and you picked it up.

RASHID
Yeah, I picked it up.

PAUL
And started to run.

RASHID
And started to run.

PAUL
(Sarcastic) Good thinking.

RASHID
That's just it. I didn't think. I just did it.

PAUL

You have one hell of a knack for getting into trouble, don't you? *(Pause, gesturing to the money)* So how much does it come to?

RASHID

Six thousand dollars. Five thousand eight hundred and fourteen dollars, to be exact.

PAUL

(Shaking his head, trying to absorb this new turn of events) So you robbed the robbers, and now the robbers are after you.

RASHID

That's it. In a nutshell.

PAUL

Yeah, well, you have to be nuts to do what you did. If you want my opinion, you should give this money back to the Creeper. Just give it back and tell him you're sorry.

RASHID

(Shaking his head) No way. There's no way I'm giving that money back. It's my money now.

PAUL

A lot of good it will do you if the Creeper finds you.

RASHID

(Stubbornly) That money is my whole future.

PAUL

Keep up with that attitude, and you won't have a future. *(Pause)* Seventeen is a hell of an age to die. Is that what you want?

Close-up of RASHID'S face. Fade out.

50. INT: DAY. THE BROOKLYN CIGAR CO.

We see RASHID mopping the floor. He finishes up and carries the mop to the bathroom behind the cash register and puts it in the bucket that is sitting in the sink. He turns on the tap and rinses the mop. Just to the side of the sink, there are two open cardboard boxes on the floor. We catch a glimpse of the contents: boxes of Montecristos (Cuban cigars). AUGGIE'S shipment from Miami has arrived.

RASHID turns off the tap, but the water continues to trickle out in a small stream into the bucket. RASHID doesn't notice.

RASHID returns to the counter. AUGGIE is standing by the door getting ready to go out. For the first time, he is clean-shaven, his hair is combed, and he is wearing dress-up clothes: a bright red plaid sports jacket, white slacks, etc. The effect is strange, laughable.

> AUGGIE
> I'll be back in about an hour. Watch the register while I'm gone, okay?

> RASHID
> Sure thing. See you later.

AUGGIE waves good-bye and leaves.

Cut to the bathroom. Close-up of the bucket in the sink. The water is overflowing, spilling onto the boxes of Cuban cigars.

Cut to the store. RASHID is sitting behind the counter, studying a picture of a naked woman in Penthouse magazine.

Cut to bathroom. Close-up of water inundating the Cuban cigars.

Cut to store. Close-up of RASHID gaping at the photograph. We hear him groan softly.

> RASHID
> (Muttering to himself) Jesus God, save me.

Dissolve.

The jarring noise of the door opening. RASHID hastily closes the magazine and stashes it under the counter. AUGGIE enters the store with two middle-aged men in dark, pin-striped suits: his lawyer-customers for the Cuban cigars.

AUGGIE

(Addressing the TWO LAWYERS as they enter. He is obviously keyed up. His manner is jovial, ingratiating) It might be illegal, but it's hard to see where the crime is if there's no victim. No harm done, right?

FIRST LAWYER

This is what it must have felt like to go to a speakeasy during Prohibition.

SECOND LAWYER

Forbidden pleasures, eh?

AUGGIE

(To RASHID) Much business while I was gone?

RASHID

A little. Not much.

AUGGIE

(To the LAWYERS) This way, gentlemen. Let's retire to my office, shall we? *(He points to the bathroom behind the counter)*

The camera stays on RASHID as AUGGIE and the LAWYERS disappear. A second later, we hear AUGGIE explode with rage.

AUGGIE (OFF)

What the fuck is going on here! Look at this! The goddamn place is flooded! Holy fucking shit! Look at this! Look at this goddamn mess!

51. INT: DAY. PAUL'S APARTMENT

Close-up of RASHID'S face. He is in tears.

PAUL (OFF)

So you lost the job. Is that what you're telling me? He just up and fired you?

RASHID

(Scarcely able to speak) It was more complicated than that. There was a reason.

PAUL (OFF)

Well?

RASHID

It wasn't my fault.

PAUL (OFF)

(Irritated) If you don't tell me what happened, how do you expect me to know that? I need facts, not opinions.

RASHID

(Struggling to speak, fighting back the tears) The water was dripping, see . . . I turned it off, but it was still dripping, and then Auggie had to go out, and so I left the back room . . . And later on . . . well, later on . . . when Auggie came back . . . the whole place was flooded. His Cuban cigars got all messed up . . . You know, soaked through . . . just when he was about to sell them . . . to these rich guys in suits. . . .

Shot of PAUL standing in the middle of the room looking at RASHID, who is sitting on the bed.

PAUL

Cuban cigars. You mean he had some hanky-panky going with those guys?

RASHID

I suppose so. He never told me about it.

PAUL

No wonder he was angry.

RASHID

He was out five thousand bucks, he said. . . . He kept saying it over and over. . . . Five thousand bucks down the drain. . . . He wouldn't stop. . . . Five thousand bucks, five thousand bucks. . . . He was like out of his mind with those five thousand bucks. . . .

Silence. PAUL paces about the room, thinking. He sits down in a chair by the table. Thinks some more.

PAUL

Here's what you're going to do. You're going to open up your backpack, take out your bag of money, count out five thousand dollars, and hand it over to Auggie.

RASHID

(Appalled) What are you talking about? *(Pause)* You can't be serious.

PAUL

I'm serious, all right. You've got to square it with Auggie. Since you won't give the money back to the Creeper, you can use it to make things right with Auggie. That's probably better anyway. Better to keep your friends than to worry about your enemies.

RASHID

(Stubbornly. Fresh tears falling down his cheeks) I'm not going to do it.

PAUL

You'll do it, all right. You fuck up, you've got to undo the damage. That's how it works, buster. If you don't do it, I'm going to throw you out of here. Do you understand me? If you don't pay Auggie what you owe him, I'm finished with you.

RASHID

I pay Auggie, and I've got nothing. Eight hundred bucks and a ticket to Shit City.

PAUL

Don't worry about it. You've got friends now, remember? Just behave yourself, and everything will work out.

52. INT: NIGHT. A BAR IN BROOKLYN

AUGGIE is sitting alone at the bar, smoking a cigarette and drinking a beer. He looks disgusted: muttering to himself, swearing under his breath. Business is slow, and the place is almost empty.

PAUL *and* RASHID *enter and approach* AUGGIE *at the bar.* RASHID *is carrying a brown paper bag.* AUGGIE *gestures with his head for them to follow him into the back room. Cut to:*

The three of them taking their seats at a table in the back room. A long, awkward pause.

PAUL

The kid's sorry, Auggie.

AUGGIE

(Scowls, fiddles with the napkin on the table) Yeah, well, I'm sorry too. *(Pause)* It took me three years to save up those five thousand bucks, and now I'm broke. I can't hardly pay for this beer. Not to speak of having my credibility destroyed. Do you understand what I'm saying? My credibility. So yeah, I'm sorry, too. About as sorry as I've ever been in my whole fucking life.

PAUL

He's got something to tell you, Auggie.

AUGGIE

If he's got something to tell me, why don't he tell it to me himself?

Without saying a word, RASHID lifts the bag off his knees and puts it on the table in front of AUGGIE. AUGGIE eyes the bag suspiciously.

RASHID

It's for you.

AUGGIE

For me? And what am I supposed to do with a paper bag?

RASHID

Open it.

AUGGIE

(Taking a peek inside) What is this, some kind of joke?

RASHID

No, it's five thousand dollars.

AUGGIE

(Disgusted) Shit, I don't want your money, you little twerp. *(Peeking inside the paper bag again)* It's probably stolen anyway.

RASHID

What do you care where it comes from? It's yours.

AUGGIE

And why the hell would you give me money?

RASHID

So I can get my job back.

AUGGIE

Your job? You've got five thousand bucks. What do you want a piece-of-shit job like that for?

RASHID

To look at the dirty magazines. I can see all the naked women I want, and it doesn't cost me a cent.

AUGGIE

You're a dumb, whacked-out little fuck, do you know that?

Auggie *pushes the bag toward* RASHID. *Without hesitating for a second,* RASHID *pushes the bag back toward* AUGGIE.

PAUL

Don't be an ass, Auggie. He's trying to make it up to you, can't you see that?

AUGGIE

(Sighs, shakes head, peeks into bag again) He's crazy.

PAUL

No, he's not. You are.

AUGGIE

(Shrugs. Begins to crack a smile) You're right. I just wasn't sure you knew.

PAUL

It's written all over you like a neon sign. Now say something nice to Rashid to make him feel better.

AUGGIE

(Peeking into the bag again. Smiles) Fuck you, kid.

RASHID

(Beginning to smile) Fuck you, too, you white son-of-a-bitch.

PAUL

(Pause. He laughs. Then, slapping his hands on the table) Good. I'm glad that's settled!

53. INT: DAY. PAUL'S APARTMENT

PAUL *is alone at his desk, typing. The keys suddenly stick, jam up.*

PAUL

(Spreading his hands in front of his face and addressing his fingers) Pay attention, boys. Look sharp.

54. INT: DAY. PAUL'S APARTMENT

Several hours later. As before: PAUL alone at his desk, typing. A loud knocking is heard at the door. PAUL continues typing. Another loud knock on the door. PAUL sighs, stands up from his desk, and leaves the work-room. Shot of PAUL walking through the big room and opening the front door. Two black men are standing in the hallway. One is very large, in his mid-thirties; the other is small, in his twenties. They are Charles Clemm, THE CREEPER, and his sidekick, ROGER GOODWIN.

> CREEPER

Mr. Benjamin, I presume?

Before PAUL can respond, CREEPER and GOODWIN push their way past him into the apartment. GOODWIN slams the door behind him. PAUL backs up nervously. He positions himself by the windows that look down at the street.

> GOODWIN

You got a security problem in this building, you know that? The lock on that door downstairs is busted.

> CREEPER

Not a good idea in these troubled times. You never know what kind of trash might wander in off the streets.

> PAUL

(Nervous) I'll talk to the landlord about it tomorrow.

> GOODWIN

You do that. Don't want no unpleasant surprises, do you?

> PAUL

(Looking them over) And who do I have the pleasure of talking to now?

> CREEPER

Pleasure? *(Laughs)* I wouldn't call this pleasure, funny man. I'd say it's more in the nature of business.

> PAUL

It doesn't matter. I know who you are anyway. *(Pause)* You're the Creeper, aren't you?

CREEPER

(Indignant) The what?

GOODWIN

(Whipping out a .45 automatic and pointing it at PAUL) Ain't nobody
calls Charles by that name to his face. *(Grabs PAUL'S arm and puts him
in a hammerlock)* Understand?

PAUL

(Grunting in pain) Sure, I understand.

*Before GOODWIN can do any real violence, the CREEPER waves him off.
At that moment, PAUL glances out the window. Shot of RASHID down on
the street, approaching the building. Shot from RASHID'S POV: We see
PAUL upstairs with his back to the window, moving his hand with a shooing gesture, trying to warn RASHID of the danger. Another shot of
RASHID'S face, puzzled. Another shot from RASHID'S POV: the CREEPER'S
head enters the picture. Another shot of RASHID: he takes off, running
down the street. As all this happens we hear the following:*

CREEPER (OFF)

Let me tell you the business we're here about. We want your cooperation

in helping us locate a certain party. We know he's been staying here, so we don't want no denials about it, understand?

                              PAUL
What party are you looking for?

                         GOODWIN (OFF)
Little Tommy Cole. A homeboy with a brain the size of a pea.

                          PAUL (OFF)
(Stalling) Tommy Cole? Never heard of him.

By now, RASHID is gone. Shot of PAUL'S face. He glances over his shoulder at the street below. Shot of the street: no sight of RASHID anywhere. Followed by a shot of PAUL, CREEPER, and GOODWIN standing in the room.

                            CREEPER
I'm not sure you heard me the first time. We *know* that boy's been here.

                              PAUL
You might think you know, but you've got the wrong information. I never heard of anyone named Tommy Cole.

                            GOODWIN
(Strolling about the room. Sees RASHID'S sketch pad on coffee table)
Lookee here, Charles. Ain't cousin Tommy fond of doodling?

He picks up the pad, flips through it, and then starts ripping up the drawings and tossing them on the floor.

                              PAUL
Hey, what the hell are you doing?

Before GOODWIN answers, CREEPER comes close to PAUL and without any warning delivers a fast, powerful punch to his stomach. PAUL doubles over in pain and falls to the floor.

                            CREEPER
So what's it going to be, funny man? Do you cooperate, or do we send you to the hospital?

GOODWIN

(*Walking toward the bookcase, addressing* PAUL *over his shoulder*) Hope
you got some good Blue Cross, baby.

GOODWIN *suddenly starts pulling books off the shelves and sweeping
them violently onto the floor.*

55. EXT: DAY. IN FRONT OF THE BROOKLYN CIGAR CO.

AUGGIE *is standing with his arm on* JIMMY ROSE'S *shoulder. We catch
them in mid-conversation.* AUGGIE *is talking;* JIMMY *is doing his best to
follow him: looking down at the ground and nodding, surreptitiously picking his nose. As they talk, we see* PAUL *walking down the street in their
direction. He is limping; one side of his face is bandaged; his left arm is in
a sling.*

AUGGIE

. . . If it happens, it happens. If it doesn't, it doesn't. Do you understand
what I'm saying? You never know what's going to happen next, and the
moment you think you know, that's the moment you don't know a
goddamn thing. That's what we call a paradox. Are you following me?

JIMMY

Sure, Auggie, I follow. When you don't know nothing, it's like paradise. I
know what that is. It's after you're dead and you go up to heaven and sit
with the angels.

AUGGIE

(*About to correct* JIMMY *when he spots* PAUL *approaching the corner*)
Jesus, man, you're one fucking mess.

PAUL

(*Shrugs*) It could have been worse. If the cops hadn't come, I might not
be standing here now.

AUGGIE

Cops? You mean they nabbed those cruds?

PAUL

No. The . . . uh . . . the Bobbsey Twins lit out when they heard the sirens. But at least they stopped playing that marimba duet on my skull. *(Pause. Smiles)* Assaultus interruptus.

AUGGIE

(Studying PAUL'S wounds) Fuckus my assus. They did some number on you.

PAUL

For once in my life I managed to keep my mouth shut. There's something to be said for that, I suppose.

JIMMY, *who has been watching PAUL intently since his arrival, gently and hesitantly raises his hand and touches PAUL'S bruised face. PAUL winces slightly.*

JIMMY

Does it hurt?

AUGGIE

Of course it hurts. What does it look like?

JIMMY

(Quietly) I thought maybe he was pretending.

PAUL

(To AUGGIE) You haven't heard from Rashid, have you?

AUGGIE

Not a peep.

PAUL

I spoke to his aunt a couple of days ago, but she hasn't heard from him either. It's beginning to get a little scary.

AUGGIE

That could be a good sign, though. It could mean that he got away.

PAUL

Or didn't. *(Pause)* There's no way of knowing, is there?

56. EXT: DAY. A BROOKLYN STREET

We see PAUL walking down the street, returning home. He spots a young black man from behind. He is wearing the same red "FIRE" T-shirt that RASHID was wearing in Scene 48. PAUL, growing excited, limps forward to catch up with him. Once he gets close enough, he taps the young man on the shoulder.

YOUNG MAN

(Wheeling around as if he had been attacked. Angrily) What the fuck you want, mister?

PAUL

(Embarrassed) I'm sorry. I thought you were someone else.

YOUNG MAN

I ain't someone else, got it? You can go fuck yourself with your someone else.

57. INT: NIGHT. PAUL'S APARTMENT

PAUL, *sitting in his easy chair, continues to work on his story by hand. The apartment has more or less been put back in order, but several traces of the CREEPER'S visit remain: bits of broken furniture, a pile of destroyed books in one corner, etc.*

After a few moments, PAUL gets up from his chair, walks over to the television set, and turns it on. We hear the crowd noises of a baseball game, the voice of the announcer describing the action, but there is no image: only a single white line across the black screen. PAUL mutters under his breath and pounds the top of the TV. An image jumps into view: a baseball game in progress. PAUL backs up to watch. The moment he steps back, the image vanishes. Once again we see the white line across the black screen. PAUL steps forward and pounds the TV again. Nothing happens. He pounds again, and still the white line remains. The camera moves in slowly for a close-up of the TV screen. The camera travels through it, into the darkness. After a moment, we hear the clicking of PAUL'S keyboard. The sounds of typing resonate in the void.

58. EXT: LATE MORNING. THE BROOKLYN PROMENADE

Sunday, late morning, brilliant sunshine. Against the backdrop of lower Manhattan, we see the summer weekend crowd along the Promenade: old people on benches reading newspapers, young couples out with their babies, girls on roller skates, boys on skateboards, bag ladies, bums. Traveling camera. Amongst the bustle of bodies and colors, we see the Brooklyn Bridge off to the right, a spider web of cables set against the buildings of upper Manhattan; to the left we see the expanse of New York Harbor, the Staten Island ferry, the Statue of Liberty. AUGGIE and RUBY are walking along the Promenade, deep in conversation. AUGGIE is clean-shaven, his hair is slicked back, and he is wearing his white pants and a bright red Hawaiian shirt. RUBY is wearing sunglasses, black toreador pants, and spike heels.

AUGGIE

So you're just going to give up and go home?

RUBY

I don't have much choice, do I? It's pretty clear she doesn't want me around.

AUGGIE

(Thinks) Still, you can't just write her off.

RUBY

Yeah? And what else am I supposed to do? There's no baby anymore, and if she wants to throw away her life, that's her business.

AUGGIE

She's just a kid. There's time for more babies later. After she grows up.

RUBY

Dream on, Auggie. She'll be lucky to make it to her nineteenth birthday.

AUGGIE

Not if you got her into one of those rehab programs.

RUBY

I'd never be able to talk her into it. And even if I could, those things cost money. And that's just what I don't have. I'm flat out dead broke.

AUGGIE

No you're not.

RUBY

(She stops) Are you calling me a liar? I'm telling you I'm broke. I don't
even have insurance on my goddamned car.

AUGGIE

(Ignoring her remark) Remember that business venture I was telling you
about? Well, my tugboat came in. I'm flush.

RUBY

(Pouting) Bully for you.

AUGGIE

No, bully for you. (He reaches into his pocket, pulls out a long white
envelope, and hands it to RUBY)

RUBY

What's this?

AUGGIE

Why don't you open it and find out?

                                RUBY

(Opens the envelope. It is filled with cash) Jesus God, Auggie. There's
money in here.

                               AUGGIE

Five thousand bucks.

                                RUBY

(Incredulous) And you're giving it to me?

                               AUGGIE

It's all yours, baby.

                                RUBY

(Moved, to the point of tears) For keeps?

                               AUGGIE

For keeps.

                                RUBY

(Now crying in earnest) I can't believe it. Oh God, I can't believe it.
(Pause, to catch her breath) You're an angel, Auggie. An angel from
heaven. *(She tries to put her arms around him, but AUGGIE squirms
away)*

                               AUGGIE

Fuck this angel shit. Just take the dough, Ruby. But no bawling, okay? I
can't stand people who blubber.

                                RUBY

I'm sorry, baby. I can't help it.

RUBY *pulls a handkerchief from her purse and blows her nose, honking
loudly.* AUGGIE *lights a cigarette. After a moment, they start walking again.*

                               AUGGIE

There's just one thing I want to know.

                                RUBY

(More composed) Anything, Auggie. Just name it.

                                1 2 0

AUGGIE *stops walking.*

> AUGGIE
>
> Felicity. *(Pause)* She's not my daughter, is she?

Long pause. Close-up of RUBY'S *face.*

> RUBY
>
> I don't know, Auggie. She might be. Then again, she might not. Mathematically speaking, there's a fifty-fifty chance. It's your call.

Close-up of AUGGIE'S *face. After a moment, he begins to smile. Fade out.*

59. EXT: DAY. SEVENTH AVENUE

We see PAUL *walking down the crowded street with a manila envelope tucked under his arm.*

60. INT: DAY. THE BOOKSTORE

We see APRIL *behind the counter. She is ringing up a sale for a CUS-TOMER, an Indian woman dressed in a sari.*

PAUL *enters the store and approaches the counter. When* APRIL *looks up and notices who it is, her face brightens—then instantly shows alarm at the sight of* PAUL'S *wounds and bandages. She completely forgets about the customer.*

> APRIL
>
> Jesus, what happened to you?

> PAUL
>
> *(Shrugging it off)* It looks worse than it is. I'm okay.

> APRIL
>
> What happened?

PAUL

I'll tell you all about it *(glancing around the store)*, but not here.

APRIL

(Pause. Shyly) It's been a while. I thought maybe you'd be in touch.

PAUL

Yeah, well, I've sort of been out of commission. *(Pause)* How's Melville?

APRIL

Almost done. A week or ten days, and I'll be there.

CUSTOMER

(Growing impatient) Miss, could I have my change, please?

APRIL

Oh, I'm sorry. *(Hands the woman her change)*

CUSTOMER

And my book.

APRIL

Sorry. *(She slips the book—Portrait of a Lady—into a bag and gives it to the woman)*

The CUSTOMER leaves, glancing over her shoulder with a disapproving look at APRIL and PAUL.

PAUL

(Extending the manila envelope to APRIL) I finished my story. I thought you might want to take a look at it.

APRIL

(Taking the envelope—and at the same moment understanding the significance of PAUL'S gesture. She begins to smile) I'd love to.

PAUL

Good. I hope you like it. It was a long time in coming.

APRIL

(*Glancing at her watch*) I get off for lunch in ten minutes. Can I treat you to a hamburger?

PAUL

(*Awkwardly*) Uh . . . actually, it might be better if you read the story first. Call me when you're finished, okay?

APRIL

(*A bit mystified, but putting a good face on her disappointment*) Okay. I'll read it tonight and call you tomorrow. (*Weighing the envelope in her hand*) It doesn't seem to be too long.

PAUL

Forty-one pages.

Another CUSTOMER—a young white man of about twenty—appears at the counter with a copy of On the Road. *PAUL begins backing toward the door.*

PAUL (cont'd)

You won't forget to call?

APRIL

I won't forget. I promise.

61. INT: NIGHT. PAUL'S APARTMENT

The telephone rings—two, three, four times—but no one is there to answer it. Cut to:

62. INT: NIGHT. THE BROOKLYN CIGAR CO.

A shot of the empty store. We hear a telephone ringing in the distance.

63. INT: NIGHT. AUGGIE'S APARTMENT

AUGGIE is sitting alone at his kitchen table, removing recently developed photographs from a yellow Kodak envelope. The 1990 album lies open on the table before him. One by one, AUGGIE affixes a small white label to the lower-right-hand corner of each image, carefully marking the date on each label with a pen: 7-30-90; 7-31-90; 8-1-90; etc. Then, one by one, he slips each photo into its appropriate place in the album. AUGGIE smokes a cigarette, hums a song under his breath, sips from a glass of bourbon. He looks like a beachcomber: unshaven, tousled hair, bare-chested, wearing a pair of baggy shorts.

The telephone is ringing. Not to be rushed, AUGGIE slides another photo into its place, takes a sip of his drink, and then, finally, answers the phone.

AUGGIE

Bureau of Missing Persons. Sergeant Fosdick. *(Pause. Listens)* Well, blow me down. Peter Rabbit's alive. *(Pause. Listens)* Yeah, that's cool. No problem. *(Pause. Listens)* Danzinger Road, Peekskill. *(Pause. Listens)* Yeah, I got it. I don't need no pencil. *(Pause. Listens)* How the hell do I know? I can't help it if he's not answering his phone. *(Pause. Listens)* So you're the one who called the cops, huh? Good work. *(Pause. Listens)* Yeah, I mean it. Good work. It probably saved his skin. *(Pause. Listens)* You got that

right. Bad. You owe him a lot, keemosabbe. *(Pause. Listens)* No, not tomorrow. I have to work, chuckle brain—remember? *(Pause. Listens)* No, not Saturday either. Sunday. *(Pause. Listens)* Yeah. Right. Okay. *(Smiles)* Yeah, and kiss my ass, too. *(Pause. Listens. Smiles again)* You, too. *(Hangs up the phone)*

64. EXT: DAY. PAUL'S STREET

Sunday morning. PAUL *and* AUGGIE *are walking together on the sidewalk.* PAUL *is carrying* RASHID'S *backpack.*

> PAUL

So what did he say when he called?

> AUGGIE

Nothing much. He said his socks and underpants were dirty, and would we mind driving up with his things. *(Pause)* Fucking kids, huh? They take you for granted every time.

AUGGIE *stops in front of a car parked at the curb: a fifteen-year-old red Coupe de Ville.*

> PAUL

(Impressed) Nice machine, Auggie. Where'd you find it?

> AUGGIE

It's Tommy's. The sucker owed me a favor.

AUGGIE *unlocks the door on the passenger side, then walks around the car to unlock the door on the driver's side.*

> PAUL

(Opening the door) It's not a long drive. An hour, an hour and a half. We'll be back in time for dinner.

> AUGGIE

We'd better be. I haven't spent a night out of Brooklyn in fourteen years, and I'm not about to break my record now. Besides, I've got to be on my corner at eight sharp tomorrow morning.

They both climb into the car. AUGGIE starts up the engine. Cut to:

65. INT/EXT: DAY. PEEKSKILL. COLE'S GARAGE

We see RASHID painting the walls in the upstairs room. The room has been transformed since the last time we saw it. It is entirely bare now and neat as a pin. With each touch of white paint that RASHID applies to the walls, the look of the place improves. He works with care, proud of what he has accomplished so far.

Suddenly: the noise of a car down below. RASHID goes to the open window and looks out. Cut to:

From RASHID'S POV: We see CYRUS, DOREEN, and JUNIOR pull up in the blue Ford. They get out. DOREEN is carrying a large picnic cooler. CYRUS opens the back door and unbuckles JUNIOR from his seat.

RASHID (OFF)

(Mumbling, alarm in his voice) Oh, Jesus. What are they doing here on Sunday?

DOREEN

(Waving up to RASHID) Hi, Paul. We decided to have a picnic. Want to join us?

Cut to RASHID at the window:

RASHID

Uh, yeah, sure. *(Pause)* Just a minute. I'll be down in a minute.

Cut to RASHID in the upstairs room. He crouches down, puts the brush he has been working with on top of the open paint can, and begins wiping his hands with a rag when, suddenly, the noise of another car is heard down below. RASHID stands up to have a look. Cut to:

From RASHID'S POV: We see the red Coupe de Ville limping into the sta-tion with a flat tire. The car stops. PAUL and AUGGIE climb out. Cut to:

Close-up of RASHID, looking out the window. His face registers panic, alarm.

RASHID

Jesus Christ!

He begins running toward the door, hoping to get downstairs to PAUL and AUGGIE before CYRUS can reach them. In his haste, he kicks over the open paint bucket.

The scene ends with a close-up of white paint oozing over the bare wood floor.

66. EXT: DAY. IN FRONT OF COLE'S GARAGE

Shot of CYRUS, DOREEN, and JUNIOR by the picnic table, unpacking their lunch. The camera pans from CYRUS—beginning to walk toward PAUL and AUGGIE—to PAUL and AUGGIE, who are standing by the gas pumps. We see PAUL and AUGGIE looking in the direction of the office, smiles beginning to form on their faces. At the precise instant CYRUS gets to them, RASHID enters the frame, panting hard from his dash down the stairs.

PAUL

(To RASHID) Hi, kid.

RASHID

(Looking at PAUL'S wounds and bandages. He is shocked) Wow. They sure did a job on you.

PAUL

Research. I worked the scene right into my story. *(Pause)* That makes the medical bills one hundred percent tax deductible.

AUGGIE

(Under his breath) Try selling that one to the IRS.

CYRUS

(Watching the exchange with a confused look on his face. To RASHID)
You know these men? *(Gesturing to the flat tire)* I thought we had some
customers.

AUGGIE

Yeah, he knows us. But you've also got some customers. *(Wheels around
and kicks the Coupe de Ville)* Fucking Tommy. Leave it to him to drive
around with bald tires.

PAUL

We came here to deliver some clean laundry.

RASHID

(To CYRUS) It's all right. I really do know them.

CYRUS

(Still confused, but trying to be friendly) I'm the owner here. Cyrus Cole.
(Extends his right hand to AUGGIE)

AUGGIE

(Shaking CYRUS'S hand) Augustus Wren.

CYRUS *extends his right hand to PAUL.*

PAUL

(Shaking CYRUS'S hand) Paul Benjamin.

Cut to close-up of RASHID'S face. The sky has just fallen on top of him.

CYRUS

(More confused than ever. Turning to RASHID) That's funny. His name is
the same as yours.

RASHID

(In a panic) Well, you and Junior have the same name, too, don't you?

CYRUS

Yeah, but he's my son. Nothing strange about that. He's my own flesh and blood. But here you got the same name as this man here, and you're not even the same *color.*

RASHID

(Improvising) That's how we met. We're members of the International Same Name Club. Believe it or not, there are 846 Paul Benjamins in America. But only two in the New York metropolitan area. That's how Paul and I got to be such good friends. We're the only ones who show up at the meetings.

AUGGIE

(Disgusted) You're full of crap, kid. Why don't you just come clean and tell the man who you are?

By now, drawn by curiosity, DOREEN has come over to where the four men are standing. She is carrying JUNIOR in her arms.

CYRUS

(Turning to PAUL) What the hell's going on, mister?

PAUL

(Shrugs, gestures to RASHID) You better ask him.

AUGGIE

Yeah, Rashid baby, spill it.

DOREEN

(In a loud voice) Rashid?

PAUL

(To DOREEN) Sometimes. It's what you'd call a *nom de guerre.*

CYRUS

(More and more confused) What the hell are we talking about?

AUGGIE

(To RASHID). Come on. Tell him your real name. The name on your birth certificate.

Close-up of RASHID'S *face. His lower lip is trembling. Tears are beginning to form in his eyes.*

                                      RASHID

(Almost inaudibly) Thomas.

                                        CYRUS

Paul. Rashid. Thomas. Which one is it?

                                      RASHID

Thomas.

                                        AUGGIE

(Impatient) Come on, come on, you yellow belly. The whole thing. First name *and* last name.

                                        RASHID

(Trying to stall. Tears begin to slide down his cheeks) What difference does it make?

                                        PAUL

If it doesn't make any difference, why not just say it?

RASHID

(To PAUL, *his voice breaking*) I was going to tell him . . . but in my own time. In my own time. . . .

AUGGIE

No time like the present, man.

CYRUS

(*To* RASHID) Well?

RASHID

(*Blinking back the tears. Looking at* CYRUS) Thomas Cole. My name is Thomas Jefferson Cole.

CYRUS

(*Thunderstruck*) Are you making fun of me? I won't be mocked. Do you hear me? I won't let no punk kid stand there and mock me!

DOREEN

(*Upset*) Cyrus!

JUNIOR

(*Reaching out to* CYRUS) Dada.

RASHID

(*Standing his ground*) Like it or not, Cyrus, that's my name. Cole. Just like yours.

PAUL

(*To* CYRUS) Now ask him who his mother was.

CYRUS

(*Beside himself*) I don't like this. I don't like it one bit.

RASHID

Louisa Vail. Remember her, Cyrus?

CYRUS

You shut your mouth! You shut your mouth now!

Unable to control his rage, CYRUS hauls off and slugs RASHID in the face. RASHID falls to the ground.

AUGGIE

(Alarmed) Hey, cut it out!

AUGGIE takes a wild swing and clips CYRUS in the mouth. DOREEN, seeing her husband attacked, gives AUGGIE a quick kick in the shins. AUGGIE lets out a yell and starts hopping up and down in pain.

DOREEN

(To AUGGIE) Damn you. There'll be none of that on my watch, you dumpy bag of shit.

DOREEN puts down JUNIOR. The little boy immediately runs over to PAUL and whacks him on his bad arm. PAUL howls in pain and drops to the ground. The whole scene is quickly degenerating into chaos.

In the meantime, RASHID has climbed back to his feet. He lines up CYRUS, rushes toward him, and tackles him to the ground. The two of them roll around on the macadam, fighting with all their strength. After a moment, it looks as though CYRUS is getting the better of the struggle. AUGGIE tries to pull them apart, but to no avail.

DOREEN (cont'd)

(Pounding CYRUS on the back with her fists) Stop it! Stop it! You'll kill him, Cyrus!

DOREEN'S shrieking voice brings the fight to a momentary halt. CYRUS rolls off RASHID and stands up. RASHID stands up as well. But the hatred between them has not subsided. CYRUS raises his hook.

DOREEN (cont'd)

(Screaming) He's your son, goddammit! He's your son! Do you want to kill your son!

Suddenly: CYRUS stops. He lowers his arm and buries his face in his right hand. A moment later, he breaks down and weeps. His sobbing makes a terrible sound: pure, animal misery. He staggers around, then falls to his knees, unable to stop the tears.

Cut to RASHID. He stands there without moving, watching CYRUS. He drops his arms to his sides, unclenches his fists. Tears are pouring down his cheeks; he is breathing hard. Close-up of his face.

Fade out.

67. EXT: DAY. THE PICNIC TABLE OUTSIDE COLE'S GARAGE

Some time later.

Long shot. We see everyone from the previous scene sitting at the picnic table eating lunch: fried chicken, lemonade, potato chips, etc. The image has the effect of a still life.

DOREEN is sitting next to CYRUS. RASHID is holding JUNIOR in his arms, gently rocking him as the child drinks milk from a bottle with his eyes closed. AUGGIE and PAUL are sitting next to each other, eating chicken and listening to DOREEN (who is the only one who has the energy to talk). CYRUS looks sullen, defeated. Every once in a while, he steals a glance at RASHID. RASHID, however, pretends to ignore him, keeping his eyes fixed on the sleeping JUNIOR.

At first we hear nothing. Then the camera moves in for a closer shot and we can begin to make out what DOREEN is saying. As she speaks, we see Paul reach into his pocket and take out a tin of his little cigars. He leans forward and offers one to CYRUS, but CYRUS reaches into his own pocket and offers PAUL a big cigar. Paul accepts and lights up. CYRUS then lights up one of his own.

DOREEN

. . . It might not have been the smartest investment, but it didn't cost much, and if Cyrus can make a go of it, we'll be able to take care of our needs. The man knows his way around cars, I'll tell you that, but the problem is this road is too far off the beaten track. Ever since they put in that mall, the traffic hasn't been too heavy around here. But you take the good with the bad, right? You do your best and hope that things work out . . .

Music begins to play. Cut to:

68. BLACK SCREEN

The music continues. After a few moments, the following words appear on the screen: "THREE MONTHS LATER."

69. EXT: DAY. ELEVATED SUBWAY, BROOKLYN

The music continues to play. We see an elevated subway train snaking along the tracks in the dim November light.

70. INT: DAY. THE BROOKLYN CIGAR CO.

AUGGIE is behind the counter, wearing a flannel shirt. The three OTB MEN are there with him, as in Scene 2. JIMMY enters the store and places a paper bag on the counter in front of AUGGIE, then slides around the counter and takes a seat beside AUGGIE. JIMMY studies his watch. AUGGIE removes a cup of take-out coffee from the bag. He lifts off the cover and steam rises from the cup. In the meantime, we see and hear the OTB MEN talking.

> TOMMY

Of course there's gonna be a war. You think they'd send five hundred thousand troops over there just to lie in the sun? I mean, there's plenty of beach, but not a hell of a lot of water. Half a million soldiers. It ain't no seaside holiday, you can bet on that.

> JERRY

I don't know, Tommy. You think anyone gives a rat's ass about Kuwait? I read something about the head sheik over there. He marries a different virgin every Friday and then divorces her on Monday. You think we want to have our kids dying for a guy like that?

> DENNIS

That's one way of upholding American values, eh, Tommy?

> TOMMY

Laugh all you want. I'm telling you there's gonna be a war. With things in Russia falling apart, those slobs in the Pentagon'll be out of work unless they find a new enemy. They got this Saddam character now, and they're going to hit him with all they've got. Mark my words.

PAUL *enters the store wearing a scarf and leather jacket. The* OTB MEN *stop talking and study him as he approaches the counter.*

> AUGGIE

(*To* PAUL) Hey, man, how's it going?

> PAUL

Hi, Auggie.

Without waiting for PAUL *to ask,* AUGGIE *turns around, pulls out two tins of Schimmelpennincks from the cigar cabinet, and places them on the counter.*

> AUGGIE

Two, right?

> PAUL

Uh, better make it one.

> AUGGIE

You usually get two.

> PAUL

Yeah, I know, but I'm trying to cut down. (*Pause*) Somebody's worried about my health.

> AUGGIE

(*Twitching his eyebrows playfully*) Ah-hah.

PAUL *shrugs with embarrassment, then slowly breaks into a warm smile.*

> AUGGIE (cont'd)

And how's the work going these days, maestro?

> PAUL

(*Still grinning. Absent-mindedly*) Fine. (*Pause. Pulling himself together*) Or

it was until a couple of days ago. A guy from *The New York Times* called
and asked me to write a Christmas story. They want to publish it on
Christmas Day.

AUGGIE

That's a feather in your cap, man. The paper of record.

PAUL

Yeah, great. The problem is, I have four days to come up with something,
and I don't have a single idea. *(Pause)* You know anything about
Christmas stories?

AUGGIE

(Blustering) Christmas stories? Sure, I know a ton of 'em.

PAUL

Anything good?

AUGGIE

Good? Of course. Are you kidding? *(Pause)* I'll tell you what. Buy me
lunch, my friend, and I'll tell you the best Christmas story you ever heard.
How's that? And I guarantee every word of it is true.

PAUL

(Smiling) It doesn't have to be true. It just has to be good.

AUGGIE

(Turning to JIMMY ROSE) Take over the register while I'm gone, okay,
Jimmy? *(Begins to extricate himself from behind the counter)*

JIMMY ROSE

You want me to do it, Auggie? You sure you want me to do it?

AUGGIE

Sure I'm sure. Just remember what I taught you. And don't let any of
these kibbitzers cause you trouble. *(Gestures to OTB MEN)* You got a
problem, you come and see me. I'll be down the block at Jack's. *(To
PAUL)* Jack's okay?

PAUL

Jack's is fine.

PAUL *and* AUGGIE *leave the store together.*

71. INT: DAY. JACK'S RESTAURANT

A cramped and boisterous kosher delicatessen with sports photographs on the walls: old Brooklyn Dodger teams, the 1969 Mets, a portrait of Jackie Robinson. PAUL and AUGGIE are sitting at a table in the back, studying the menus.

PAUL

(Closing menu) I have to pee. If the waiter comes, order me a corned beef on rye and a ginger ale, okay?

AUGGIE

You got it.

PAUL *stands up and leaves to go to the men's room. Alone at the table,* AUGGIE *glances down at the empty chair next to him and sees a copy of* The New York Post. *The paper is open to an article with a headline that reads:* "SHOOTOUT IN BROOKLYN." AUGGIE *bends over to inspect the article more closely. Close-up of the article. We see photographs of CHARLES CLEMM (the CREEPER) and ROBERT GOODWIN and their names in the captions. A secondary headline reads:* "ROBBERS KILLED IN JEWEL HEIST." *In the meantime, as* AUGGIE *continues to study the article, the* WAITER *arrives to take his order. He is a round, balding, middle-aged man with a weary expression on his face.*

WAITER (OFF)

What'll it be, Auggie?

AUGGIE

(Looking up) Uh . . . *(pointing to* PAUL'S *empty place)* my friend over here would like a corned beef on rye and a ginger ale.

Shot of WAITER *holding pencil and order pad.*

WAITER

And what about for you?

AUGGIE

(*Reading the paper again. Suddenly remembers the* WAITER *is there*)
Huh?

WAITER

What about for you?

AUGGIE

For me? (*Pause*) I'll have the same thing. (*Looks down at the article
again*)

WAITER

Do me a favor, will you?

AUGGIE

(*Glancing up again*) What's that, Sol?

WAITER

Next time, when you want two corned beef sandwiches, say, "Two
corned beef sandwiches." When you want two ginger ales, say, "Two
ginger ales."

AUGGIE

What's the difference?

WAITER

It's simpler, that's what. It makes things go faster.

AUGGIE

(*Mystified. Humoring the* WAITER) Uh, sure, Sol. Anything you say.
Instead of saying, "One corned beef sandwich," and then, "Another
corned beef sandwich," I'll say, "Two corned beef sandwiches."

WAITER

(*Deadpan*) Thanks. I knew you'd understand.

The WAITER *leaves.* AUGGIE *looks down at the article again.* PAUL *returns and sits down in his chair across from* AUGGIE.

                              PAUL
(Settling in) So. Are we ready?

                             AUGGIE
Ready. Any time you are.

                              PAUL
I'm all ears.

                             AUGGIE
Okay. *(Pause. Thinks)* You remember how you once asked me how I started taking pictures? Well, this is the story of how I got my first camera. As a matter of fact, it's the only camera I've ever had. Are you following me so far?

                              PAUL
Every word.

                             AUGGIE
(Close-up of AUGGIE'S *face)* Okay. *(Pause)* So this is the story of how it happened. *(Pause)* Okay. *(Pause)* It was the summer of 'seventy-six, back when I first started working for Vinnie. The summer of the bicentennial. *(Pause)* A kid came in one morning and started stealing things from the store. He's standing by the rack of paperbacks near the front window stuffing skin magazines under his shirt. It was crowded around the counter just then, so I didn't see him at first. . . .

AUGGIE'S *face dissolves into* PAUL'S. *Black-and-white footage begins: we see* AUGGIE *acting out the events he describes to* PAUL. *This scene exactly duplicates the events shown earlier in Scenes 2 and 3—with one difference. The thief is now* ROGER GOODWIN, *the same person who beat up* PAUL *in Scene 54, the same person whose picture* AUGGIE *has just noticed in the newspaper. The events unfold in silence, accompanied by* AUGGIE'S *voice-over narration.*

                     AUGGIE (VOICE-OVER)
But once I noticed what he was up to, I started to shout. He took off like a jackrabbit, and by the time I managed to get out from behind the

counter, he was already tearing down Seventh Avenue. I chased after him for about half a block, and then I gave up. He'd dropped something along the way, and since I didn't feel like running anymore, I bent down to see what it was.

We see AUGGIE chasing the kid, giving up, and bending down for the wallet. He starts walking back to the store.

AUGGIE (VOICE-OVER)

It turned out to be his wallet. There wasn't any money inside, but his driver's license was there, along with three or four snapshots. I suppose I could have called the cops and had him arrested. I had his name and address from the license, but I felt kind of sorry for him. He was just a measly little punk, and once I looked at those pictures in his wallet, I couldn't bring myself to feel very angry at him. . . .

We see AUGGIE examining the pictures. Close-ups of the pictures.

AUGGIE (VOICE-OVER)

Roger Goodwin. That was his name. In one of the pictures, I remember, he was standing next to his mother. In another one, he was holding some trophy he got from school and smiling like he just won the Irish Sweepstakes. I just didn't have the heart. A poor kid from Brooklyn

without much going for him, and who cared about a couple of dirty magazines, anyway? . . .

Cut to Jack's Restaurant. The WAITER *arrives at the table with their orders.*

WAITER

Here you go, boys. Two corned beef sandwiches. Two ginger ales. The fast way. The simple way. *(He leaves)*

PAUL

(Putting mustard on his sandwich) And?

AUGGIE

(Taking a sip of his drink) So I held onto the wallet. Every once in a while I'd get a little urge to send it back to him, but I kept delaying and never did anything about it. *(Puts mustard on his sandwich)* Then Christmas rolls around, and I'm stuck with nothing to do. Vinnie was going to invite me over, but his mother got sick, and he and his wife had to go down to Florida at the last minute. *(Takes a bite of the sandwich, chews)* So I'm sitting in my apartment that morning, feeling a little sorry for myself, and then I see Roger Goodwin's wallet lying on a shelf in the kitchen. I figure what the hell, why not do something nice for once, and I put on my coat and go out to return the wallet. . . .

Cut to black-and-white footage: the housing projects in Boerum Hill. We see AUGGIE *wandering alone among the buildings, bundled up against the cold. At the same time, we hear:*

AUGGIE (VOICE-OVER)

The address was over in Boerum Hill, somewhere in the projects. It was freezing out that day, and I remember getting lost a few times trying to find the right building. Everything looks the same in that place, and you keep going over the same ground thinking you're somewhere else. Anyway, I finally get to the apartment I'm looking for and ring the bell. . . .

Shot of AUGGIE *walking down a corridor in the housing projects; graffiti on the cinder-block walls. He stops in front of a door and pushes the buzzer.*

AUGGIE (VOICE-OVER)

Nothing happens. I assume no one's there, but I try again just to make
sure. I wait a little longer, and just when I'm about to give up, I hear
someone shuffling to the door. An old woman's voice asks, "Who's there?"
and I say I'm looking for Roger Goodwin. "Is that you, Roger?" the old
woman says, and then she undoes about fifteen locks and opens the
door. . . .

*Shot of a very old black woman, GRANNY ETHEL, opening the door. A
rapturous, expectant smile is on her face. Even though the scene unfolds
in silence, we see AUGGIE and GRANNY ETHEL mouthing the dialogue
that AUGGIE repeats to PAUL.*

AUGGIE (VOICE-OVER)

She has to be at least eighty, maybe ninety years old, and the first thing I
notice about her is she's blind. "I knew you'd come, Roger," she says. "I
knew you wouldn't forget your Granny Ethel on Christmas." And then she
opens her arms as if she's about to hug me.

*We see AUGGIE hesitate for a second. As he reports the next little part of
the story, we see him giving in, opening his arms, and hugging GRANNY
ETHEL. The hug is then repeated in somewhat slower motion; then again*

in slow motion; then again, in very slow motion; then again in motion so
slow that it appears as a sequence of still photographs.

AUGGIE (VOICE-OVER)

I don't have much time to think, you understand. I had to say something
real fast, and before I knew what was happening, I could hear the words
coming out of my mouth. "That's right, Granny Ethel," I said. "I came
back to see you on Christmas." Don't ask me why I did it. I don't have
any idea. It just came out that way, and suddenly this old woman's
hugging me there in front of the door, and I'm hugging her back. It was
like a game we both decided to play—without having to discuss the
rules. I mean, that woman *knew* I wasn't her grandson. She was old and
dotty, but she wasn't so far gone that she couldn't tell the difference
between a stranger and her own flesh and blood. But it made her happy
to pretend, and since I had nothing better to do anyway, I was happy to
go along with her. . . .

AUGGIE and GRANNY ETHEL enter the apartment and sit down in chairs
in the living room. We see them talking, laughing. Meanwhile, we hear:

AUGGIE (VOICE-OVER)

So we went into the apartment and spent the day together. Every time
she asked me a question about how I was, I would lie to her. I told her I'd

found a good job in a cigar store, I told her I was about to get married, I told her a hundred pretty stories, and she made like she believed every one of them. "That's fine, Roger," she would say, nodding her head and smiling. "I always knew things would work out for you. . . ."

The camera pans slowly through GRANNY ETHEL'S apartment, lingering momentarily on various objects. Among other things, we see portraits of Martin Luther King, Jr., John F. Kennedy, family photographs, balls of yarn, knitting needles. By the time this visual tour is completed, we see AUGGIE entering the apartment again, wearing his coat and carrying a large bag of groceries. As described in the simultaneous narration:

AUGGIE (VOICE-OVER)

After a while, I started getting hungry. There didn't seem to be much food in the house, so I went out to a store in the neighborhood and brought back a mess of stuff. A precooked chicken, vegetable soup, a bucket of potato salad, all kinds of things. Ethel had a couple of bottles of wine stashed in her bedroom, and so between us we managed to put together a fairly decent Christmas dinner. . . .

We see AUGGIE and GRANNY ETHEL at the dining-room table: eating the food, drinking the wine, talking.

AUGGIE (VOICE-OVER)

We both got a little tipsy from the wine, I remember, and after the meal was over we went out to sit in the living room where the chairs were more comfortable. . . .

We see AUGGIE leading GRANNY ETHEL by the arm and helping her into a chair. Then AUGGIE leaves the living room and walks to the bathroom down the hall.

AUGGIE (VOICE-OVER)

I had to take a pee, so I excused myself and went to the bathroom down the hall. That's where things took another turn.
It was ditsy enough doing my little jig as Ethel's grandson, but what I did next was positively crazy, and I've never forgiven myself for it. . . .

We see AUGGIE in the bathroom. As he pees, we see the boxes of cameras, just as he describes them.

AUGGIE (VOICE-OVER)

I go into the bathroom, and stacked up against the wall next to the shower, I see a pile of six or seven cameras. Brand-new, thirty-five-millimeter cameras, still in their boxes. I figure this is the work of the real Roger, a storage place for one of his recent hauls. I've never taken a picture in my life, and I've certainly never stolen anything, but the moment I see those cameras sitting in the bathroom, I decide I want one of them for myself. Just like that. And without even stopping to think about it, I tuck one of the boxes under my arm and go back to the living room. . . .

We see AUGGIE return to the living room with the camera. GRANNY ETHEL is sleeping soundly in her chair. AUGGIE puts the camera down, clears the table, and washes the dishes in the kitchen.

AUGGIE (VOICE-OVER)

I couldn't have been gone for more than three minutes, but in that time Granny Ethel had fallen asleep. Too much Chianti, I suppose. I went into the kitchen to wash the dishes, and she slept on through the whole racket, snoring like a baby. There didn't seem to be any point in disturbing her, so I decided to leave. I couldn't even write a note to say good-bye, seeing that she was blind and all, so I just left. I put her

grandson's wallet on the table, picked up the camera again, and walked out of the apartment. . . .

We see AUGGIE *bending over the sleeping* GRANNY ETHEL *and deciding not to wake her. We see him put the wallet on the table and pick up the camera. We see him walking out of the apartment. Shot of the closing door.*

                         AUGGIE (VOICE-OVER)
And that's the end of the story.

Cut to PAUL'S *face.* PAUL *and* AUGGIE *are sitting at the table, eating the last bites of their sandwiches.*

                              PAUL
Did you ever go back to see her?

                             AUGGIE
Once, about three or four months later. I felt so bad about stealing the camera, I hadn't even used it yet. I finally made up my mind to return it, but Granny Ethel wasn't there anymore. Someone else had moved into the apartment, and he couldn't tell me where she was.

                              PAUL
She probably died.

                             AUGGIE
Yeah, probably.

                              PAUL
Which means that she spent her last Christmas with you.

                             AUGGIE
I guess so. I never thought of it that way.

                              PAUL
It was a good deed, Auggie. It was a nice thing you did for her.

                             AUGGIE
I lied to her, and then I stole from her. I don't see how you can call that a good deed.

PAUL

You made her happy. And the camera was stolen anyway. It's not as if the person you took it from really owned it.

AUGGIE

Anything for art, eh, Paul?

PAUL

I wouldn't say that. But at least you've put the camera to good use.

AUGGIE

And now you've got your Christmas story, don't you?

PAUL

(Pause. Thinks) Yes, I suppose I do.

PAUL *looks at* AUGGIE. *A wicked grin is spreading across* AUGGIE's *face. The look in his eyes is so mysterious, so fraught with the glow of some inner delight, that* PAUL *begins to suspect that* AUGGIE *has made the whole thing up. He is about to ask* AUGGIE *if he has been putting him on—but then stops, realizing that* AUGGIE *would never tell him.* PAUL *smiles.*

                         PAUL (cont'd)
Bullshit is a real talent, Auggie. To make up a good story, a person has to know how to push all the right buttons. *(Pause)* I'd say you're up there among the masters.

                         AUGGIE
What do you mean?

                         PAUL
I mean, it's a good story.

                         AUGGIE
Shit. If you can't share your secrets with your friends, what kind of friend are you?

                         PAUL
Exactly. Life just wouldn't be worth living, would it?

AUGGIE *is still smiling.* PAUL *smiles back at him.* AUGGIE *lights a ciga-rette;* PAUL *lights a little cigar. They blow smoke into the air, still smiling at each other.*

The camera follows the smoke as it rises toward the ceiling. Close-up of the smoke. Hold for three, four beats.

The screen goes black. Music begins to play.

Final credits.

auggie wren's christmas story

I heard this story from Auggie Wren. Since Auggie doesn't come off too well in it, at least not as well as he'd like to, he's asked me not to use his real name. Other than that, the whole business about the lost wallet and the blind woman and the Christmas dinner is just as he told it to me.

Auggie and I have known each other for close to eleven years now. He works behind the counter of a cigar store on Court Street in downtown Brooklyn, and since it's the only store that carries the little Dutch cigars I like to smoke, I go in there fairly often. For a long time, I didn't give much thought to Auggie Wren. He was the strange little man who wore a hooded blue sweatshirt and sold me cigars and magazines, the impish, wisecracking character who always had something funny to say about the weather or the Mets or the politicians in Washington, and that was the extent of it.

But then one day several years ago he happened to be looking through a magazine in the store, and he stumbled across a review of one of my books. He knew it was me because a photograph accompanied the review, and after that things changed between us. I was no longer just another customer to Auggie, I had become a distinguished person. Most people couldn't care less about books and writers, but it turned out that Auggie considered himself an artist. Now that he had cracked the secret of who I was, he embraced me as an ally, a confidant, a brother-in-arms. To tell the truth, I found it rather embarrassing. Then, almost inevitably, a moment came when he asked if I would be willing to look at his photographs. Given his enthusiasm and goodwill, there didn't seem to be any way I could turn him down.

God knows what I was expecting. At the very least, it wasn't what Auggie showed me the next day. In a small, windowless room at the back of the store, he opened a cardboard box and pulled out twelve identical black photo albums. This was his life's work, he said, and it didn't take him more than five minutes a day to do it. Every morning for the past twelve years, he had stood at the corner of Atlantic Avenue and Clinton Street at precisely seven o'clock and had taken a single color photograph of precisely the same view. The project now ran to more than four thousand photographs. Each album represented a different year, and all the pictures were laid out in sequence, from January 1 to December 31, with the dates carefully recorded under each one.

As I flipped through the albums and began to study Auggie's work, I didn't know what to think. My first impression was that it was the oddest, most bewildering thing I had ever seen. All the pictures were the same. The whole project was a numbing onslaught of repetition, the same street and the same buildings over and over again, an unrelenting delirium of redundant images. I couldn't think of anything to say to Auggie, so I continued turning pages, nodding my head in feigned appreciation. Auggie himself seemed unperturbed, watching me with a broad smile on his face, but after I'd been at it for several minutes, he suddenly interrupted me and said, "You're going too fast. You'll never get it if you don't slow down."

He was right, of course. If you don't take the time to look, you'll never manage to see anything. I picked up another album and forced myself to go more deliberately. I paid closer attention to details, took note of shifts in the weather, watched for the changing angles of light as the seasons advanced. Eventually, I was able to detect subtle differences in the traffic flow, to anticipate the rhythm of the different days (the commotion of workday mornings, the relative stillness of weekends, the contrast between Saturdays and Sundays). And then, little by little, I began to recognize the faces of the people in the background, the passers-by on their way to work, the same people in the same spot every morning, living an instant of their lives in the field of Auggie's camera.

Once I got to know them, I began to study their postures, the way they carried themselves from one morning to the next, trying to discover their moods from these surface indications, as if I could imagine stories for them, as if I could penetrate the invisible dramas locked inside their bodies. I picked up another album. I was no longer bored, no longer puzzled as I had been at first. Auggie was photographing time, I realized, both natural time and human time, and he was doing it by planting himself in one tiny corner of the world and willing it to be his own, by standing guard in the space he had chosen for himself. As he watched me pore over his work, Auggie continued to smile with pleasure. Then, almost as if he had been reading my thoughts, he began to recite a line from Shakespeare. "Tomorrow and tomorrow and tomorrow," he muttered under his breath, "time creeps on its petty pace." I understood then that he knew exactly what he was doing.

That was more than two thousand pictures ago. Since that day, Auggie and I have discussed his work many times, but it was only last week that I learned how he acquired his camera and started taking pictures in the first place. That was the subject of the story he told me, and I'm still struggling to make sense of it.

Earlier that same week, a man from the *New York Times* called me and asked if I would be willing to write a short story that would appear in the paper on Christmas morning. My first impulse was to say no, but the man was very charming and persistent, and by the end of the conversation I told him I would give it a try. The moment I hung up the phone, however, I fell into a deep panic. What did I know about Christmas? I asked myself. What did I know about writing short stories on commission?

I spent the next several days in despair, warring with the ghosts of Dickens, O. Henry and other masters of the Yuletide spirit. The very phrase "Christmas story" had unpleasant associations for me, evoking dreadful outpourings of hypocritical mush and treacle. Even at their best, Christmas stories were no more than wish-fulfillment dreams, fairy tales for adults, and I'd be damned if I'd ever allowed myself to write something like that. And yet, how could anyone propose to write an unsentimental Christmas story? It was a contradiction in terms, an impossibility, an out-and-out conundrum. One might just as well try to imagine a racehorse without legs, or a sparrow without wings.

I got nowhere. On Thursday I went out for a long walk, hoping the air would clear my head. Just past noon, I stopped in at the cigar store to replenish my supply, and there was Auggie, standing behind the counter as always. He asked me how I was. Without really meaning to, I found myself unburdening my troubles to him. "A Christmas story?" he said after I had finished. "Is that all? If you buy me lunch, my friend, I'll tell you the best Christmas story you ever heard. And I guarantee that every word of it is true."

We walked down the block to Jack's, a cramped and boisterous delicatessen with good pastrami sandwiches and photographs of old Dodgers teams hanging on the walls. We found a table at the back, ordered our food, and then Auggie launched into his story.

"It was the summer of seventy-two," he said. "A kid came in one morning and started stealing things from the store. He must have been about nineteen or twenty, and I don't think I've ever seen a more pathetic shoplifter in my life. He's standing by the rack of paperbacks along the far wall and stuffing books into the pockets of his raincoat. It was crowded around the counter just then, so I didn't see him at first. But once I noticed what he was up to, I started to shout. He took off like a jackrabbit, and by the time I managed to get out from behind the counter, he was already tearing down Atlantic Avenue. I chased after him for about half a block, and then I gave up. He'd dropped something along the way, and since I didn't feel like running anymore, I bent down to see what it was.

"It turned out to be his wallet. There wasn't any money inside, but his driver's license was there along with three or four snapshots. I suppose I could have called the cops and had him arrested. I had his name and address from the license, but I felt kind of sorry for him. He was just a measly little punk, and once I looked at those pictures in his wallet, I couldn't bring myself to feel very angry at him. Robert Goodwin. That was his name. In one of the pictures, I remember, he was standing with his arm around his mother or grandmother. In another one, he was sitting there at age nine or ten dressed in a baseball uniform with a big smile on his face. I just didn't have the heart. He was probably on dope now, I figured. A poor kid from Brooklyn without much going for him, and who cared about a couple of trashy paperbacks anyway?

"So I held onto the wallet. Every once in a while I'd get a little urge to send it back to him, but I kept delaying and never did anything about it. Then Christmas rolls around and I'm stuck with nothing to do. The boss usually invites me over to his house to spend the day, but that year he and his family were down in Florida visiting relatives. So I'm sitting in my apartment that morning feeling a little sorry for myself, and then I see Robert Goodwin's wallet lying on a shelf in the kitchen. I figure what the hell, why not do something nice for once, and I put on my coat and go out to return the wallet in person.

"The address was over in Boerum Hill, somewhere in the projects. It was freezing out that day, and I remember getting lost a few times trying to find the right building. Everything looks the same in that place, and you keep going over the same ground thinking you're somewhere else. Anyway, I finally get to the apartment I'm looking for and ring the bell. Nothing happens. I assume no one's there, but I try again just to make sure. I wait a little longer, and just when I'm about to give up, I hear someone shuffling to the door. An old woman's voice asks who's there, and I say I'm looking for Robert Goodwin. 'Is that you, Robert?' the old woman says, and then she undoes about fifteen locks and opens the door.

"She has to be at least eighty, maybe ninety years old, and the first thing I notice about her is that she's blind. 'I knew you'd come, Robert,' she says. 'I knew you wouldn't forget your Granny Ethel on Christmas.' And then she opens her arms as if she's about to hug me.

"I didn't have much time to think, you understand. I had to say something real fast, and before I knew what was happening, I could hear the words coming out of my mouth. 'That's right, Granny Ethel,' I said. 'I came back to see you on Christmas.' Don't ask me why I did it. I don't have any idea. Maybe I didn't want to disappoint her or something, I don't know. It just came out that way, and then this old woman was suddenly hugging me there in front of the door, and I was hugging her back.

"I didn't exactly say that I was her grandson. Not in so many words, at least, but that was the implication. I wasn't trying to trick her, though. It was like a game we'd both decided to play—without having to discuss the rules. I mean, that woman *knew* I wasn't her grandson Robert. She was old and dotty, but she wasn't so far gone that she couldn't tell the difference between a stranger and her own flesh and blood. But it made her happy to pretend, and since I had nothing better to do anyway, I was happy to go along with her.

"So we went into the apartment and spent the day together. The place was a real dump, I might add, but what else can you expect from a blind woman who does her own housekeeping? Every time she asked me a question about how I was, I would lie to her. I told her I'd found a good job working in a cigar store, I told her I was about to get married, I told her a hundred pretty stories, and she made like she believed every one of them. 'That's fine, Robert,' she would say, nodding her head and smiling. 'I always knew things would work out for you.'

"After a while, I started getting pretty hungry. There didn't seem to be much food in the house, so I went out to a store in the neighborhood and brought back a mess of stuff. A precooked chicken, vegetable soup, a bucket of potato salad, a chocolate cake, all kinds of things. Ethel had a couple of bottles of wine stashed in her bedroom, and so between us we managed to put together a fairly decent Christmas dinner. We both got a little tipsy from the wine, I remember, and after the meal was over we went out to sit in the living room, where the chairs were more comfortable. I had to take a pee, so I excused myself and went to the bathroom down the hall. That's where things took yet another turn. It was ditsy enough doing my little jig as Ethel's grandson, but what I did next was positively crazy, and I've never forgiven myself for it.

"I go into the bathroom, and stacked up against the wall next to the shower, I see a pile of six or seven cameras. Brand-new thirty-five-millimeter cameras, still in their boxes, top-quality merchandise. I figure this is the work of the real Robert, a storage place for one of his recent hauls. I've never taken a picture in my life, and I've certainly never stolen anything, but the moment I see those cameras sitting in the bathroom, I decide I want one of them for myself. Just like that. And without even stopping to think about it, I tuck one of the boxes under my arm and go back to the living room.

"I couldn't have been gone for more than a few minutes, but in that time Granny Ethel had fallen asleep in her chair. Too much Chianti, I suppose. I went into the kitchen to wash the dishes, and she slept on through the whole racket, snoring like a baby. There didn't seem to be any point in disturbing her, so I decided to leave. I couldn't even write a note to say good-bye, seeing that she was blind and all, and so I just left. I put her grandson's wallet on the table, picked up the camera again, and walked out of the apartment. And that's the end of the story."

"Did you ever go back to see her?" I asked.

"Once," he said. "About three or four months later. I felt so bad about stealing the camera, I hadn't even used it yet. I finally made up my mind to return it, but Ethel wasn't there anymore. I don't know what happened to her, but someone else had moved into the apartment, and he couldn't tell me where she was."

"She probably died."

"Yeah, probably."

"Which means that she spent her last Christmas with you."

"I guess so. I never thought of it that way."

"It was a good deed, Auggie. It was a nice thing you did for her."

"I lied to her, and then I stole from her. I don't see how you can call that a good deed."

"You made her happy. And the camera was stolen anyway. It's not as if the person you took it from really owned it."

"Anything for art, eh, Paul?"

"I wouldn't say that. But at least you've put the camera to good use."

"And now you've got your Christmas story, don't you?"

"Yes," I said. "I suppose I do."

I paused for a moment, studying Auggie as a wicked grin spread across his face. I couldn't be sure, but the look in his eyes at that moment was so mysterious, so fraught with the glow of some inner delight, that it suddenly occurred to me that he had made the whole thing up. I was about to ask him if he'd been putting me on, but then I realized he would never tell. I had been tricked into believing him, and that was the only thing that mattered. As long as there's one person to believe it, there's no story that can't be true.

"You're an ace, Auggie," I said. "Thanks for being so helpful."

"Any time," he answered, still looking at me with that maniacal light in his eyes. "After all, if you can't share your secrets with your friends, what kind of a friend are you?"

"I guess I owe you one."

"No you don't. Just put it down the way I told it to you, and you don't owe me a thing."

"Except the lunch."

"That's right. Except the lunch."

I returned Auggie's smile with a smile of my own, and then I called out to the waiter and asked for the check.

blue in the
face

"this is brooklyn.
we don't go by numbers"

Blue in the Face is not a sequel to *Smoke*. Although it draws on settings and characters from that film, it sprints off in an entirely new direction. Its spirit is comic; its engine is words; its guiding principle is spontaneity. As producer Peter Newman aptly put it when first presented with the idea: it's a project in which the inmates take over the asylum.

The original plan for *Blue in the Face* was far simpler than the swirling free-for-all it eventually became. The premise was to go back into the cigar store that appears at the beginning and end of *Smoke* and create a little portrait of Auggie Wren's world. Minor characters from the first film would become major characters in the second. Besides Auggie, just one other major character from *Smoke* would participate—but only in a minor role.

Our approach to all this was primitive in the extreme. We would invent situations for these characters and have each one last the length of a roll of film, approximately ten minutes. Two takes per scene would be sufficient, we felt. One to warm up and then another to get it right. We would present each skit as a chapter, continuous and uncut, and add musical interludes between the chapters for the sake of variety. With only three days of filming available to us, we didn't see how there would be time for much else.

The notes I prepared for the actors were written in extreme haste, literally dashed off in the time it took to put the words on paper. Their sole purpose was to rough out the general contents of each scene, and they were never meant to be anything more than crude signposts, a rapid shorthand to remind us of what we thought we were supposed to be doing. Even as I typed them up, I knew that everything was subject to change.

Not only were we asking the actors to improvise their lines, we were counting on them to create entire scenes without any rehearsals. The success or failure of the film was in their hands, and we had to give them absolute freedom to go where they wanted to go.

Most of the situations were cooked up in the back seat of a car—riding downtown in evening traffic after the *Smoke* dailies. Wayne and I would throw out ideas to each other at random: What if? . . . How about? . . . What do you think of? . . . We figured that we would need eleven or twelve scenes, both as a minimum and a maximum. As a minimum because we knew in advance that much of what we shot wouldn't work, and we didn't want to get caught with too little material. As a maximum because we didn't think it would be possible to shoot more than four scenes a day.

Miramax gave the go-ahead in early June. *Smoke* was in the middle of production then, and so while Wayne went to the set every day to work on that film, I met with the actors in restaurants and offices around town to prepare for the other. Little by little, new actors joined the cast and new roles had to be devised for them (Dot, Pete, Bob, et al.), but our basic approach remained the same: give the performers their marks, turn on the camera, and see what happened.

What happened proved to be fairly extraordinary. Some scenes failed, some actors were better at improvising than others, but by and large everyone performed at an astonishingly high level. We accumulated nine or ten hours of footage during those three days (July 11, 12, 13), and the minute we saw the results, we knew that we would have to throw our original conception of the film out the window. Situations would have to be broken up, a new and complex order of scenes would have to be found, and when normal editing devices didn't work, we would have to resort to jumpcuts, dissolves, and other little tricks to keep the action moving.

It was at this point that editor Chris Tellefsen became a full partner in the enterprise. Working closely with Wayne and myself, he shaped the material we gave him into the wild and wooly film it now is. There was no script to follow, no plot to rely on, no preordained structure to help simplify decisions. It was all a matter of instinct, of understanding the strengths and weaknesses of the original footage, and then drawing on those strengths to assemble the finished movie. Wayne and I spent countless hours in the cutting room with Chris, trying out scores of different ideas in an ongoing triangular conversation, and his energy and patience were unflagging. In every sense of the word, he is a co-author of the film.

What this film is, however, is difficult to pin down. Yes, it's funny. Yes, it's vulgar and rambunctious and silly—and to see it as anything other than a high-spirited celebration of daily life in Brooklyn would be a serious mistake. And yet, for all its nonsense, I believe there's something in *Blue in the Face* that makes it more than just a frivolous diversion. A certain rawness, perhaps. A certain way of rolling with the punches that's best summed up in the line Giancarlo Esposito delivers to Lily Tomlin: "This is Brooklyn. We don't go by numbers," People smoke like chimneys, people argue, people get in each other's faces. They roll up their sleeves and yell, they insult each other, they say obnoxious things. Nearly every scene in *Blue in the Face* is about conflict. The characters are embattled, highly opinionated, relentless in their anger. And yet, when all is said and done, the film is genuinely amusing, and one walks away from it with a feeling of great human warmth. I find that interesting. Perhaps that means a certain degree of conflict is good for us. Perhaps we need an occasional release from all the high-minded pieties that tell us how we're supposed to talk to each other. I'm not saying this is so, but it's definitely a question worth pondering.

However you want to describe it, the film we put together from those three days of shooting turned out to be much richer and funnier than we were expecting. There were obvious weak spots, but all in all the experiment had paid off. When we screened it in October for our backers, Harvey and Bob Weinstein, they responded enthusiastically. Good as they felt it was, however, they were convinced it could be even better. It was hard to disagree with them. They offered to finance another three days of shooting, and the moment we left their office, the mad scramble to go back into production began. The actors and crew had to be reassembled, new actors had to be hired, replacements for certain jobs had to be found, and it all had to be done in no time flat. Our main actor, Harvey Keitel, was leaving the country in nine days to begin work on another film, and he wouldn't be returning to New York for several months. It was now or never.

Somehow, we managed to pull it off, and on October 27 we all went back to the cigar store for another round of shooting. We wrapped the following Monday, Halloween. By the time we were ready to leave the set, it was dark outside, and the Brooklyn streets were filled with children dressed in costumes. Some of them, mistaking the Brooklyn Cigar Company for an actual store, wandered in to ask for candy. The store itself might have been make-believe, but it had real candy in it, and so we filled the kids' trick-or-treat bags with chewing gum and chocolate bars from the shelves. It seemed like a fitting way to say good-bye to our imaginary world, the perfect ending for *Blue in the Face*.

December 29, 1994

notes for the actors

july

1. Philosophers

Cast: the Macanudo Lady, Auggie, Jimmy Rose, Tommy, Jerry, Dennis

Dennis walks into the store and tells the following story: "Yesterday after-noon, I was walking down Seventh Avenue and saw this little twelve-year-old kid snatch a woman's purse. He just grabbed it off her shoulder and started tearing down the street. A lot of people were around, but nobody did anything, and there's this woman (not a bad-looking chick, I might add) screaming her lungs out on the sidewalk: 'Thief! Thief! He stole my purse!' So, upstanding citizen that I am, I take off after the kid. I finally nab the sucker a couple of blocks down the avenue . . . and then drag him back to the woman. At the very least, I figure I'll get a date with her for my act of heroism. At least a little hug or a kiss on the goddam cheek. By now a big crowd has gathered around the woman to see what all the fuss is about. 'Here he is,' I say to her, giving her back her purse, 'here he is, now let's call the cops.' But the bitch takes one look at him and says, 'I can't do it. He's too young. I can't be responsible for sending him to jail. He's just a baby.'

"This really pisses me off. After all I've done for her! Not only have I worked myself into a sweat, but I tore my goddamn shirt reaching for the kid . . . (points to his armpit) right here. Brand-new shirt that was, one hundred percent silk. Cost me eighty-eight fucking dollars. 'Listen, lady,' I say to her, 'it's your duty as a citizen to call the cops. Is this the kind of city you want to live in? Where little kids are ripping off people's purses—and getting away with it? It's people like you who are turning New York into such a shit-hole.

You won't take responsibility!' But she wouldn't back down. 'I won't do it,' she kept saying. 'I won't do it. He's just a child.'

"I was feeling pretty burned by now. Not only was I not going to see any action with this broad, but I'd chased the kid for nothing. So you know what I did? I ripped the purse out of the woman's hands and gave it back to the thief. Talk about a confused look. The kid was so frightened and mixed up by then, I thought he was going to shit his pants. 'Go on,' I said to him, 'it's yours. Get out of here. Just take it and go.' And, believe it or not, the kid went. He took off running down the street, just like before, and this time no one ran after him."

The others react and give their opinions. Auggie thinks Dennis did exactly the right thing. Tommy thinks Dennis should have gone to the cops himself. Jerry, expressing sympathy for the thief, says Dennis never should have chased him in the first place.

The men argue back and forth. The situation becomes more and more heated. Just when it is about to degenerate into a full-scale shouting match, an elegant woman in her thirties or forties enters the store . . .

WOMAN (To) A tin of Macanudos, please.
AUGGIE Your husband must like this brand a lot. This is about the tenth time you've come in this summer for Macanudos.
WOMAN My husband?
AUGGIE I don't mean to be nosey.
WOMAN Of course not. But my husband doesn't smoke. And besides, I'm not married to him anymore. Just to keep the record straight.
AUGGIE Oh.
WOMAN Just to keep the record straight, these babies are for me.

Jimmy Rose watches this exchange with growing wonder. He is smitten, head-over-heels in love with the Macanudo Lady. Just as she is about to leave:

JIMMY Miss . . . can I ask you a question?
WOMAN Of course . . .
JIMMY Would you let me kiss you . . . on the lips?
WOMAN What!
JIMMY Don't worry. We'll get married later. But first I want to see if you kiss good.

Just as Auggie begins to scold Jimmy for his crude behavior, the Macanudo Lady recovers her poise and gives Jimmy a kiss. Then she leaves the store.

A long discussion follows about sex and love. Everyone puts in his two cents, including Jimmy, who keeps repeating, "But that's what you guys always say." Tommy is the most amused. He commends Jimmy on his ability to say what he means. "I've wanted to say that to a hundred women on the street. I just haven't had the guts."

> The incident described in this scene is based on a real event. I heard it from my wife more than ten years ago, and it has stayed with me ever since: the quintessential New York tale, a story that embodies the social and moral dilemmas of contemporary urban life . . . with a weirdly comic twist.
>
> From the very start, we knew that this would be the first scene in the film. Not only would it capture the tone we wanted, but it would present the basic cast of characters and give a taste of everyday life in the cigar store. Unfortunately, this scene was shot early on the first day, before we abandoned our arbitrary rule of two takes per scene. The actors were still warming up, and even though much good work was generated by the performances, the story of the woman's purse never emerged with sufficient clarity. *Philosophers* was edited in fifty-seven different ways, and no one was ever satisfied with the results. The failure of this episode was the primary reason for shooting again in October.
>
> As for the Macanudo Lady, we filmed that bit as a separate scene—but the results were equally disappointing. The Macanudo Lady had been a minor character in *Smoke*, but I had cut her out of the script in the final draft. It seemed like a good idea to resurrect her for *Blue in the Face*, but whatever it was we were hoping for never quite materialized on screen.

2. Belgian Waffles

Cast: the Belgian Waffle Man, Jerry, Tommy, Dennis, Violet, John Lurie and his two drummers

A scruffy panhandler is posted outside the door of the Brooklyn Cigar Company. One by one, Auggie and the three OTB Men come out, and one by one he asks them the same question: "Excuse me, sir. Could you spare four dollars and ninety-five cents? That's how much I need for a Belgian waffle and one scoop of pistachio ice cream. Right now, that's the only thing in the world I want. I want it so bad, I can't stand it anymore. A Belgian waffle . . . with one big scoop of pistachio ice cream."

First encounter: Jerry. He's sympathetic, but he doesn't have a penny. Turns his pockets inside out to prove it.

Second encounter: Tommy. He tells him to get lost.

Third encounter: Dennis. He lectures the bum on the evils of sugar. "I'll give you a couple of bucks for a Big Mac," he says, "but I know you'll use them to buy that waffle, and I don't want to contribute to diabetes and heart disease."

Fourth encounter: Auggie. At first he resists, but the bum's appeal is so strange and his manner so bizarre that he eventually gives in and hands the guy a buck. The Waffle Man is very touched and grateful. "Thank you, kind sir," he says. "A few more people like you, and maybe my dream will come true. *(Pause)* Hey, that rhymes, doesn't it? *(Recites):* A few more people like you/And maybe my dream will come true!"

He wanders off, reciting the poem to himself.

A moment later, Violet appears. She kisses Auggie on the cheek.

AUGGIE Hey, Violet. You like Belgian waffles?
VIOLET Belgian waffles? You think I want to eat that crap and mess up a body like this? Forget those Belgian waffles, Auggie. I give you a French kiss instead.
AUGGIE Right here?
(They kiss).
VIOLET You remember those steps I taught you last week, Auggie?
AUGGIE Sure, sure. One-two-three, one-two-three.
VIOLET Let's see.
(He demonstrates; she instructs)

John Lurie and his two drummers are sitting in chairs on the sidewalk with their instruments. Lurie is grinning from ear to ear.

AUGGIE What are you smiling about?
LURIE You're about the worst dancer I ever saw.

AUGGIE Yeah, well, it's hard to dance without any music. Gotta feel the beat.
VIOLET Yeah. Can you guys play a rhumba?

They start playing. Violet and Auggie dance. After a few moments, the musicians stop. Lurie says to Auggie: "Music or no music, you're still the worst dancer I ever saw."

The Belgian Waffle Man was another minor character cut from the screen-play of *Smoke*—and, once again, the scene is based on a real event. I met the Waffle Man on a Brooklyn street corner about five years ago. The pitch he delivered to me was precisely the one I put in the notes, word for word.

What impressed me most about him was his determination, the absolute specificity of what he was after. Here was a man who knew what he wanted, and no matter how many people he had to beg from, no matter how many hours or days it took him, he was going to get that Belgian waf-fle. Since then, the words "Belgian waffle" have been fraught with meaning for me. They are a metaphor for patience and single-mindedness, for day-dreams and the pursuit of pleasure, for the irreducible quirkiness of human desires.

However simple the Waffle Man's role might have been, we had a great deal of trouble finding an actor to play it. One person said yes and then backed out, and then a couple of other performers turned us down. Time was running short, and it began to look as if we would have to scratch the scene. Then, just days before we were supposed to start filming, Lily Tomlin accepted the role. Over the course of one weekend, I must have talked on the telephone with her four or five times. The first idea was for her to play it as a woman, but when I told her that wasn't strictly necessary, she decided to do it as a man. Everything about her character she prepared herself: the cos-tume, the voice, the hair, everything. She flew in from Los Angeles the night before she was scheduled to work, arrived on the set early in the morning, and immediately went to the wardrobe trailer to put on her costume. And once she was in costume, she was in character. She wasn't Lily Tomlin any-more, she was the Waffle Man—even between takes. Looking back on it now, I'm astonished by what she was able to do with such skimpy mater-ial—a few little hints, really. What I gave her was no more than a nursery song, and she turned it into a full-scale aria.

The last part of the scene, when Violet appears and dances with Auggie, was wholly successful. Mel Gorham never made a false move in any of her scenes, and when the film consisted of just the three days from July, that segment was part of it. It was cut out later for reasons of overall structure, not performance.

3. War Wounds

Cast: Tommy, Auggie

Tommy walks into the store just as Auggie is closing up for the day. He says he has some bad news and didn't want to break it over the phone. Auggie invites him in. . . .

Tommy says that his brother Chuck died last night. "I got the news this morning. Heart attack. He was drinking a glass of beer and just keeled over."

Auggie is stunned. "But he's only 46, 47 years old. People don't die at that age."

Over the course of the conversation, we learn that Auggie and Chuck were good friends in the navy—which explains how Tommy and Auggie know each other.

Auggie reminisces about the old days: about how Chuck once busted someone in the face for calling him a nigger; about his luck at poker, his laugh, his fondness for girls named Wanda. Then Auggie launches into a story about how Chuck saved him one night in a bar in Manila.

Tommy talks about how Chuck never really recovered from the war; about how fat he became; about his trouble holding a job; about his broken marriage. "My big brother," he says over and over again. "My big brother. . . ."

Tommy asks Auggie if he'll get up and say a few words at the funeral. Auggie agrees. . . .

> One take only. It came at the end of the last day, and everyone was hot, exhausted, ready to fall on the ground. Given the other material we had filmed, it seemed clear that this scene wouldn't survive the final cut—but we decided to film it anyway. It turned out to be a harrowing twelve or fourteen

minutes. Harvey and Giancarlo both wept, and the emotional intensity of their performances moved everyone who was there. But (as predicted) the tone didn't match up with the other scenes in the movie, and the entire effort wound up on the cutting-room floor.

4. Rhumba Rumble

Cast: Auggie, Dot, Violet

Auggie is alone in the store, doing inventory. Dot (Vinnie's wife) enters. She complains about Vinnie . . .

DOT He don't talk to me no more.
AUGGIE You've been married to him for fifteen years—and you still expect him to talk to you?
DOT I've given him fifteen years of my life, and all I get for it is cold, blank stares.
AUGGIE And a ranch house in Massapequa. And a white Caddy. And those doodads arounds your neck.
DOT It's not worth it. I'm sorry you ever introduced me to him, Auggie. It was the biggest mistake of my life.
AUGGIE *(Playful)* Well, you had your chance with me, but you went with the bucks . . . and not with the buck!
DOT Come on, Auggie, this is serious. I've got to talk to you.
AUGGIE Listen, Dot, Vinnie's my friend. I don't want to get involved in this. It's not right for me to start choosing sides.

Before they can go any farther, Violet enters . . . and Dot exits the store.

Violet reminds Auggie of their date to go dancing on Saturday night. Auggie has forgotten and made other plans.

AUGGIE I thought it was *next* Saturday.
VIOLET Bullshit, Auggie. We said the sixteenth. What kind of number you trying to pull on me?
AUGGIE I promised Tommy I'd help him clean out his brother's apartment. Chuck. We were in the navy together. He died a couple of days ago.
VIOLET I don't know what you're talking about. Chuck, Chuck. Who the fuck is Chuck?
AUGGIE Come on, we'll do it next week.

VIOLET You two-timing, baby, ain't you? Who is it? Dot? Sally? Or maybe that little waitress with the fat ass.

Auggie grows increasingly irritated, defensive . . . but then, suddenly, Violet begins to turn on the charm. She dances a rhumba for Auggie, and after a while he joins in. One thing leads to another, and they wind up on the floor behind the counter. . . .

Roseanne was the first "outside" actor we asked to be in *Blue in the Face.* Until then, our plan had been to limit the cast to people who had been in *Smoke,* but when we heard that she might be interested in playing a role for us, we didn't hesitate to ask her in. That was how Dot was born—literally overnight.

Roseanne was out of the country just then, but I talked with her on the phone a couple of times to discuss her role. Right from the start, she seemed to have a strong intuitive grasp of the kind of film we were proposing to make. Wayne and I had dinner with her in New York the night before shooting began (just two days after *Smoke* was finished), and even though Roseanne wasn't scheduled to work until the second day, she came to the set the next morning and wound up staying through lunch—getting the lay of the land, so to speak, soaking up the atmosphere. That same night, she got together with Harvey Keitel and Victor Argo, and the three of them worked out many of the major issues they would be wrestling with in *Blackjack.* By the next day, she was ready to go, and her first scene went extremely well in every take.

5. It's a Steal

Cast: Charles Clemm, Auggie, Tommy, Vinnie

Charles Clemm enters the store. In his present guise, he is working as a fence. He carries a briefcase filled with stolen watches, which he tries to sell to Auggie and Tommy at bargain prices.

But things don't go well. Tommy doubts the watches are authentic and taunts Clemm. After keeping up a good face, Clemm begins to get annoyed. He launches into a diatribe against smoking. "You're killing people in this store, you know that? You call me a thief, but you guys are murderers."

The tension mounts. Race becomes an issue. In his anger, Clemm turns on Tommy and says, "What are you doing here, man? You think you're white or something?"

Just when it looks as if the argument might come to blows, Vinnie enters the store and asks what the trouble is. "Nothing," Auggie says. "We were waiting for you to show up and sing us a song."

After some prompting, Vinnie takes out his guitar and sings a sad country-western ballad.

> Nothing went quite as planned, but everything worked out better than expected. Malik Yoba is a whirlwind, and at first I was thrown off by the bluster and contentiousness of his performance. I doubted it would play well on screen, but I was wrong. That bluster and contentiousness lie at the very heart of the film.
> Incredibly enough, the little song Malik sings with the guitar was made up *on the spot.*

6. The Bosco Foundation

Cast: Tommy, Pete

Tommy is sitting alone in a chair outside the cigar store, idly perusing a newspaper. A man walks by carrying a briefcase. He is Peter Malone, a former high school classmate of Tommy's. They haven't seen each other in fifteen or twenty years. . . .

PETE Tommy Fratello, right?
TOMMY Right. And you're . . . you're . . . *(snaps fingers)* Peter Malone. The whiz kid of Midwood High.

They begin to talk. Tommy asks Pete what he's been up to all these years, and Pete tells his story. Little by little, it becomes clear that Pete is out of his mind.

PETE I got my B.A. at Harvard, and then I went to Yale for my Ph.D. Interdisciplinary studies: philosophy and biology.
TOMMY *(Impressed)* Wow. And then what?
PETE Uh, I went away.

TOMMY Away?

PETE Yeah. Government research. Top-secret stuff. Uh, I'm not really supposed to talk about it.

(It's beginning to dawn on Tommy that Pete was in a mental hospital.)

Tommy asks Pete what he's doing now, and Pete tells him that he's working as a consultant for the Bosco Foundation.

TOMMY Bosco? Isn't that the chocolate milk we used to drink as kids?

PETE That's a different Bosco. You never heard of Giuseppe Bosco, the industrialist from Milan? You're half Italian, aren't you?

TOMMY Yeah, well, I'm a little out of touch with things in the old country.

PETE Bosco invented the electronic Bible. He made millions with it, and after he died, his children set up an international social research foundation. Basically, we're out to explore people's attitudes about themselves and the world and see if we can't help to make them happier.

TOMMY And how do you do that?

PETE Well, for one thing we ask people to answer questions.

TOMMY Interesting. What kind of questions?

(Pete opens his briefcase and begins removing folders filled with sloppily arranged papers.)

PETE Look, if you're not too busy, maybe you wouldn't mind doing one of the questionnaires with me now.

TOMMY Right here?

PETE Sure, right here. It won't take long.

TOMMY Okay, why not? Fire away, Pete.

During the course of the questioning, Pete becomes increasingly overwrought. The ten questions are:

1. Do you believe there is life on other planets—or that we are alone in the universe?
2. Is there anyone you hate enough to want dead? If someone told you he could kill that person for you and the crime would never be discovered, would you allow him to go ahead and do it?
3. Do you think professional athletes are overpaid?
4. Are you satisfied with the size and shape of your penis?
5. Do you believe in God?

6. Do you look at your bowel movements before you flush the toilet?
7. If a genie came to you and offered to grant you one wish, what would that wish be?
8. Where is the most unusual place you have had sex?
9. If you were President of the United States, name three changes you would make.
10. How much money would it take for you to eat a bowl of shit?

As Tommy answers, Pete frantically transcribes what he says in a notebook. Tommy understands that Pete is not right in his head and that there is no such thing as the Bosco Foundation, but he nevertheless answers the questions seriously. He feels sorry for Pete and does his best to play along. When he hears the last question, he smiles and shakes his head.

TOMMY Every man has his price, huh? Well, it won't work with me, Pete. Eating shit is against my religion.
PETE Oh? And what religion is that?
TOMMY The religion of sanity. You should think about converting. It would make your life a hell of a lot easier.
PETE Oh, I used to belong. But they excommunicated me. (*Laughs, then grows serious. Starts putting the papers back in the briefcase*) Thank you for your cooperation, Tommy. (*Stands up and shakes Tommy's hand*)

You've been a great help in the cause of truth and happiness. And don't worry about a thing. Your answers will be kept in strictest confidence.

Pete bounces off with zest. Tommy remains in his chair, watching his old high school friend walk down the street.

This scene was a last-minute addition, an afterthought. The production was already set, the notes had been written, all the actors had been talked to (except the Waffle Man, who still had to be found), when all of a sudden I was told that Michael J. Fox had joined the cast. Would it be possible for me to write a role for him? To tell the truth, I didn't think so. I was dead tired, and whatever crazy impulse had driven me to concoct the other situations had long since vanished. I was a novelist, not a gag writer, and I was in no mood to whip up another dumb comedy sketch. The only thing I wanted was to spend a quiet Fourth of July weekend at home with my family, catching up on my sleep.

But it had to be done, and Saturday and Sunday were both ruined for me. I felt burned out, disgusted, and couldn't come up with a single idea. All the scenes had been mapped out, the balance of characters had been established, and adding another player to the mix threatened to throw everything out of whack. On Monday, my wife Siri patiently listened to my complaints. We discussed several possibilities, none of them very promising, and then, out of the blue, she tossed me the idea of the questionnaire. That got me going again, and a few hours later the Bosco Foundation scene was finished.

A couple of days later, Michael J. Fox drove up to the set of *Smoke* in Garrison, New York, where the last week of shooting was underway. I was impressed by his enthusiasm for the project, his intelligence, his goodwill. Whatever reluctance I felt about adding the scene had completely vanished by the time he drove off. That night, I spoke to Giancarlo Esposito on the phone, and the Bosco Foundation was slotted in as the first scene to be shot on the second day.

As chance would have it, the second day turned out to be my first day as director. Wayne had come down with bronchitis in Garrison during the last days of *Smoke*. He stayed in bed over the weekend (coming out only briefly on Sunday night for dinner with Roseanne) and showed up on the set Monday morning. All the scenes for that day were to be shot indoors. The air conditioner had to be turned off for the sound recording, and with temperatures outside close to a hundred degrees, it was utterly stifling inside the store. By the afternoon, it was becoming difficult to breathe in there. Wayne pushed on through the day, but he clearly wasn't up to par, and by the end of the afternoon he had lost his voice and was sick as a dog. He called Peter Newman from home that evening and said that he wouldn't be able to make it on Tuesday. "Paul can do it," he said to Peter, "there won't be a problem."

He couldn't possibly know that, of course, but it was nice of him to say it. So I stepped in for the next two days and did what I could. The first scene up was *The Bosco Foundation*, and all three takes went like gangbusters. I was lucky. Fox, Esposito, and Harris were a great combination, and everyone on the crew was very kind to me, especially Adam Holender (the director of photography) and Todd Pfeiffer (the assistant director). The only problem was my inability to say the word "cut." For the first couple of takes, when I wanted Adam to stop shooting I lowered my arm in a kind of quick chopping motion. Adam didn't see this, of course, so the film kept rolling. It took a couple of shoves from Todd to get me to open my mouth. As I told Peter Newman after the scene was over, it was difficult for me to use an old word in a new way. Until that morning, the only time I had ever said "cut" was when I looked down at my finger and saw blood trickling out of it.

7. Blackjack

Cast: Auggie, Dot, Vinnie

Outline: Auggie is alone in the store when Dot enters. She unburdens her-self to him and tells of her plan to leave Vinnie and run off to Las Vegas to become a blackjack dealer. She tries to entice Auggie to go with her. Even-tually, Vinnie enters. It turns out that the deed for the store is made out in Dot's name, which makes her the legal owner of the Brooklyn Cigar Com-pany. Vinnie and Dot get into a shouting match. Auggie throws them both out.

Suggestions:

DOT Listen, Auggie, you've really got to hear me out. No funny business this time.

AUGGIE Give me a break, Dot. I don't want to get involved.

DOT Well, like it or not, you *are* involved, and I'm not leaving this store until you listen to me.

AUGGIE Okay, okay. But make it short. I've got work to do. There's a big shipment coming within the hour.

DOT I'm leaving Vinnie.

AUGGIE I've heard that one before.

DOT This time I'm serious. I'm leaving Vinnie.

AUGGIE And what about the kids? You're just going to leave them behind?

DOT They don't need me. They're old enough to take care of themselves. And besides, they don't even like me. Goddamn brats, they can live with their father. Let him take care of them for a change.

AUGGIE And where are you going to go?

DOT That's what I want to talk to you about.

AUGGIE Me? What's this got to do with me?

DOT I want you to come with me, Auggie. We'll go out West and start a new life together.

AUGGIE What!

DOT I've got it all planned out. We'll go to Vegas and work as blackjack dealers. Enough of Brooklyn, enough of Long Island. It's time for a little glitz.

AUGGIE (*Looking at her as if she's crazy*) And you've told Vinnie about this plan of yours?

DOT Not yet. I wanted to hear what you said first.

AUGGIE Yeah, well, I say you're nuts.

DOT Come on, Auggie, just stop and think about it a little. (*Growing flirta-tious, seductive*) Just because I made the wrong choice when I was young, that don't mean I can't make the right choice when I'm . . . when I'm . . . mature.

AUGGIE I'm already seeing someone. You know that. If Violet ever gets wind of this conversation, she'll scratch your eyes out. And my eyes, too.

DOT Don't be a wuss, Auggie. Forget that floozy chiquita. I know you've still got the hots for me.

AUGGIE Come on, Dot. Cut it out. You and Vinnie are in a lull, that's all. You'll get back on track.

DOT Don't make me laugh. We've been in a "lull" for the past fifteen years.

AUGGIE He's crazy about you. He tells me that all the time. "I love that chubby broad as much as I did the day I married her." He tells me that all the time.

DOT Bullshit, Auggie. Any moron could see through that one.

VINNIE enters the store.

VINNIE (*To DOT*) There you are. I've been looking all over for you.

DOT I'm having a private conversation with Auggie, Vin. Scram.

VINNIE This is my store, ain't it? I can come in here whenever I want.

DOT Think again, o beloved spouse. The papers for this place are in my name. Don't you remember that little tax scam you set up with your accountant two years ago? It's my store now, and I want you out.

Dot and Vinnie start to argue. Auggie tries to stop them, but with no suc-cess. At last, he yells at them both and tells them to leave. He has work to do, and if they want to have a domestic quarrel, they should do it at home. Dot and Vinnie head for the door, but then Dot rushes back and kisses Auggie passionately on the lips.

DOT (To AUGGIE) Too bad, pal. You just said good-bye to the opportunity of a lifetime. I hope you live to regret it.

> This scene was a struggle. We went through seven takes, trying out a differ-ent approach each time, all of us sweltering in the mid-afternoon heat. The pressure to come up with something usable was enormous, and there were moments in the beginning when I felt close to desperation. Nothing seemed to be developing as I'd hoped it would. By the third or fourth take, however, things took a turn for the better, and good material slowly started to emerge: Roseanne's shrieks, the kiss, the argument about listening and communica-

tion, Vic's anger and confusion, Harvey's magnificent smile at the end. Something real was happening in that room, and much of what is good about the scene crystalized as the camera was turning. The original idea was that Dot would go off to Las Vegas alone, but Roseanne's performance was so persuasive, her need to go there so powerful, that she actually talked Vic into going with her. No one was prepared for that, which probably explains why that moment is so convincing. It just happened, in the same way that most of life just happens.

All three actors worked extremely hard, but of all the scenes I directed, this was the one I felt least in control of. I look back on the experience as a kind of mental slugfest. Nevertheless, in its finished form, it stands as one of the strongest sequences in the film.

8. Sweet Farewell

Cast: Bob, Auggie, Jimmy Rose

Bob enters the store. Auggie asks him where he's been: he hasn't seen him in a couple of months. In Japan, Bob says: there was an exhibition of his photographs in Tokyo. Auggie asks Bob if he wants a pack of Luckies (Bob's usual brand). No, Bob says. What's the matter, Auggie answers, you switch to something else after all these years? No, Bob says, he's trying to quit. In fact, he's down to his last cigarette—and that's why he's come into the store: to smoke his last cigarette with Auggie.

Bob sits down, takes the cigarette out of the pack, and holds it in his hand. For the rest of the scene, he alternately addresses Auggie, Jimmy, and the cigarette.

A monologue follows. Memories of smoking. From the first cigarette as a kid to the final puff as an adult. Smoking and sex. Smoking and food. Smoking and work. As Schoenberg once said when asked why he kept a cigarette burning on his desk while he worked: "Composition is a lonely business, and I like it there for the companionship." Smoking and tension. Smoking and relaxation. There's never a bad time for a smoke: you celebrate with a smoke, you mourn with a smoke. Smoke as thought, as contemplation, as action. Smoking as danger: sneaking smokes in the school bathroom, smoking as a constant reminder of your own mortality. Smoking as comaraderie, as love: sharing a cigarette with your woman in bed. Smoking as the last act: the last puff before they blindfold the man about to be executed by the firing squad. Each puff is a human breath. Each puff is a thought. Each puff is another reminder that to live is also to die.

Bob strikes a match and lights the cigarette.

> The part of the man who comes into the store to smoke his last cigarette was originally conceived for William Hurt. Unfortunately, he wasn't available on the day we needed him, so Paul the novelist exited the scene, and Bob the photographer (Jim Jarmusch) stepped into his shoes.
> Jim and I went out for dinner one night in a restaurant near the *Smoke* production office on Lafayette Street, and in a couple of hours we came up with dozens of additional ideas for his part. The fact that Jim is a dyed-in-the-wool cigarette smoker lent an unforced authenticity and conviction to his performance. Not only is he a fine director, he is a complete natural in front of the camera.
> I had always thought of this scene as a pure monologue, but Jim and Harvey played it more as a conversation. This led to a number of interesting digressions, particularly Harvey's memory of *A Walk in the Sun*, which in turn led us to find a clip from the old Richard Conte movie and weave it into the film. . . .

9. Cowboys and Indians

Cast: Sue, Dennis, Auggie, Tommy, Jerry, Jimmy Rose

Background: Sue is a waitress in a diner down the street. Dennis goes out with Sue's younger sister, Mary. Sue is divorced from Phil. Phil and Dennis occasionally work together (scalping tickets).

Sue comes into the store and asks Auggie for a pack of Kools. She spots Dennis.

SUE Don't you have anything better to do than hang around here all day?
DENNIS *(Sarcastically)* Hi, Sue.
SUE Mary told me you stood her up last night. Good work, pea brain. I still can't figure out why a sister of mine would hang out with a low-life like you.

The insults go back and forth, gradually gaining in intensity. At one point, DENNIS mentions that Phil complained that she was frigid.

SUE Yeah, well, you try going to bed with someone who hasn't taken a bath since the first Nixon administration.
DENNIS That's not the way I heard it.

Sue becomes so upset that she walks over to Dennis and slaps him. Auggie and Tommy scold Dennis for being a putz.

Jimmy Rose, feeling sorry for Sue, walks over to her and gives her a hug. "Don't feel bad," he says. "I'm rigid, too. Just like him." He points to the cigar store Indian standing by the door. Jimmy's comment is so loopy, so off the mark, that Sue begins to laugh through her tears.

Dennis leaves in disgust.

The scene ends with Jimmy doing imitations of the wooden Indian.

One of our tactics in preparing *Blue in the Face* was to give each of the actors secrets, private information that was withheld from the other actors in the scene. The hope was to inspire spontaneity in the performances, to make the action seem as "real" as possible. There were times when this method backfired on us and the actors were unintentionally working at cross-purposes, but there were other times when it was crucial to the success of the scene. *Cowboys and Indians* is probably the best example of what happens when the secret is a good one. Dennis (Steve Gevedon) had no idea that

Sue (Peggy Gormley) was going to slap him. Since Dennis is the most obnoxious character in the film, Steve was instructed to insult Peggy without mercy, to go at her with every ounce of his unsavory Brooklyn manhood— but that was all he was told. When the slap came, it took him utterly by surprise. The look on his face was genuine, and yet somehow or other Steve managed to stay in character, even as he registered his shock.

10. Threads

Cast: Tommy, Jerry

Tommy and Jerry are sitting in chairs outside the store. Tommy is disgusted with Jerry. "You're turning into a loser," he says, "a vacant lot with weeds growing in it." Jerry says he's doing his best. "I'm not a sharp guy like you."

Tommy looks at Jerry's vest. It's a complicated fisherman's thing, with a hundred little pockets. Strings of different colors are hanging out of the pockets and safety-pinned to the shoulders. "What's with this vest?" he says.

Jerry explains. He keeps forgetting things. So now he has a special compartment for each object he carries: a pocket for sunglasses, a pocket for cigarettes, a pocket for his lighter, his penknife, his chewing gum, etc.— with a different string attached to each object. It's all color-coded, he says. Once you know that blue means cigarettes and red means lighter, you can't make a mistake and reach into the wrong pocket. He gives a long-winded, infinitely detailed exegesis on the system he has developed.

Tommy, growing bored and frustrated, breaks in and lectures him on how to dress well and the importance of looking good.

> This scene was essentially a holdover from the first idea for the film, before we decided to open up the cast to include actors who had not appeared in *Smoke*. Giancarlo gave a splendid performance as a man expatiating on the values of dressing well. He looked like a million dollars in his bright yellow jacket, and from start to finish he radiated strength, happiness, and self-assurance. Alas, this scene did not fit into the overall design of the film, but one can catch a glimpse of Giancarlo and his jacket in the credit sequence at the end.

11. Oy Vegas

Cast: Auggie, Tommy, Jerry, Dennis, Jimmy Rose, Vinnie

Absolute silence. Auggie is reading a book behind the counter. Tommy is reading a newspaper. Jerry is playing with the strings on his vest. Dennis is dozing off. Jimmy Rose is dusting the wooden Indian. A long moment. Vinnie enters the store in a foul mood. He reprimands Auggie for letting the OTB Men hang out in the store without buying anything. He shoos them out. Jimmy goes on with his dusting.

Once they're alone, Auggie asks Vinnie what's wrong. Dot's disappeared, that's what's wrong. Did she leave a note? Yeah, one word: Good-bye.

AUGGIE What'd you do to her, Vin?
VINNIE I didn't do nothing. She's crazy, that woman. Sick in the head.
AUGGIE Then maybe you're lucky to be rid of her.
VINNIE She's my wife. And besides, I can't take care of the kids myself. They're driving me nuts.
AUGGIE Call around. Maybe she's at her mother's.
VINNIE I did. I called her mother, her sister, her brother, her goddamn aunts and uncles, her mah-jongg partners . . . and no one's heard from her.
AUGGIE Try Vegas.
VINNIE You mean Las Vegas?
AUGGIE Oy Vegas.
VINNIE Shit, Auggie, that's not funny.
AUGGIE No, I mean it. That's where she told me she wanted to go. To become a blackjack dealer.

The conversation continues. Eventually:

VINNIE Well, I guess I'm going to Vegas, then.
AUGGIE Don't forget to take your guitar, Vinnie. Maybe you can get a gig or two while you're out there.
VINNIE *(Thinks)* You know, that's not a bad idea. Take a little break from the ratrace. Maybe I could catch on with one of those little clubs. . . .

A bit later:

VINNIE Why don't you come with me, Auggie? We'll have a blast.

AUGGIE I can't. And besides, I don't want to.

VINNIE I hate to think of you turning into an old man sitting behind that counter.

AUGGIE Don't worry about me. Everybody has to grow old. What difference does it make where it happens?

This scene was never filmed. Because Dot managed to talk Vinnie into going to Las Vegas with her, the material became superfluous.

12. Once More, With Feeling

Cast: Charles Clemm, Tommy, Jerry, Dennis, Auggie, Jerry, Jimmy Rose

Charles Clemm enters the store. This time he is dressed in an elegant three-piece suit and speaks with an upper-class Jamaican accent. He asks for pipe tobacco.

Tommy stares at him, recognizing him from the previous scene. "You're no Jamaican," he says. "You're that fence who came in here last week trying to sell those watches." Clemm smiles: "I got tired of that routine. I figured it was time to try out a new one." Dennis is impressed: "Say, you're pretty good. You totally fooled me with that voice." Clemm: "That's nothing. I've got a hundred more where that came from."

For the rest of the scene, Dennis, Tommy, Clemm, and Auggie try out different accents, dazzling each other with their extraordinary mimicry. The whole thing ends in laughter.

Another near disaster, shot on the first day. The idea for the scene had come to me on the set of *Smoke*. Separately, and on several different occasions, both Steve Gevedon and Malik Yoba had put me in stitches with their ability to do accents—everything from Japanese to Jamaican. It seemed fitting to end the film with everyone in the store impersonating everyone else, but the plan didn't work. We shot two unsuccessful takes, and then Wayne and I went into a corner and frantically tried to come up with a new approach. Then we split up and talked to the actors individually, giving each one fresh guidelines. I remember standing with Giancarlo, throwing out different suggestions for a story he could tell Malik. The one he actually used was completely his own—whether real or invented I don't know. Not only did it settle down the scene and give some shape to the action, but the content of the story touched on many of the same subjects presented in *Philosophers*. Beyond just helping to save this particular scene, his little tale of crime and redemption enriched the film as a whole.

13. Interview with Jimmy Rose

Because we had to work at top speed, all of the scenes were shot in masters. There was no time to do any of the coverage shots that are standard practice when making a movie—and which prove invaluable when editing material in the cutting room. One of our plans was to use the last hour of the last day to shoot some singles and close-ups of Jimmy Rose (Jared Harris), as well as a number of inanimate objects in the cigar store: the wooden Indian, the cash register, the window, etc. Unfortunately, when the time came to film these bits, the electric generator broke down (because of the heat, I suppose) and we no longer had any lights. We hastily decided to post Jared in a chair outside the store and ask him a number of questions: Jimmy Rose on love, on life, on the various characters who pass in and out of the store. Jared came through with an excellent performance, but after we studied the film the next day, we all agreed that the light was too dim. When we returned to the cigar store in October, we shot the interview again.

14. Interview with Lou Reed

I had met Lou Reed the previous year, and in the meantime we had struck up the beginnings of a friendship. When Wayne and I started preparing *Blue in the Face,* it occurred to me to ask Lou to participate. I don't know exactly why. Something to do with his caustic sensibility, perhaps, his appreciation of the ironies of life, or perhaps simply because of his marvelous New York-accented voice. Whatever the reason, Wayne liked the idea as well.

We decided to use Lou as himself, not as an actor: just sit him behind the counter of the cigar store and get him to talk on various subjects. He was to be the resident philosopher of the Brooklyn Cigar Company, a man who just happened to be there, for no particular reason, expounding on this and that. We looked on his presence as a possible way to break up the dramatic scenes and give some variety to the film, but we had no clear idea as to how that might happen.

The interview was shot at the end of the second day, directly after the tumultuous and draining experience of filming *Blackjack* with Roseanne, Harvey, and Vic. I was so tired by then that I could barely open my mouth to ask Lou the questions. We shot twenty-five or thirty minutes of footage, and all during that time I remember thinking that Lou was flat, not at all in good form, and that none of it would make the final cut of the film. Lou was of exactly the same opinion. We walked back to my house together for a drink after the day's work was done, and we both felt disappointed, shaking our heads and trying to shrug it off. "Well, that's show business," we said, and then went on to talk about other things.

As everyone who has seen the film now knows, show business proved us both wrong. At every *Blue in the Face* screening I have attended, Lou's performance provokes the most laughter and the most comments. He steals the movie.

october

1. EXT: DAY. IN FRONT OF THE BROOKLYN CIGAR CO.

AUGGIE *and* VIOLET *are standing in front of the store.* AUGGIE *seems distracted. As* VIOLET *talks to him, his eyes scan the street, as if searching for a lost thought.*

VIOLET Okay, Auggie, you got it?
AUGGIE Yeah, I got it.
VIOLET Saturday the sixteenth.
AUGGIE Right.
VIOLET It's gotta be then, 'cause that's the only night Ramon and his band are playing in Brooklyn. He's my brother, Auggie, and I'm telling you, he's the best.
AUGGIE Don't worry, sweetheart. It's a date.
VIOLET You gonna be something else, Agosto. Just remember those steps I taught you, and you'll look like Fred fucking Astaire.
AUGGIE *(Smiling)* Okay, Ginger. Whatever you say.

At that moment, coming around the corner to the right of frame, we see a black BOY *of about eleven and a white* WOMAN *in her late twenties. The* BOY *grabs the* WOMAN'S *purse and starts running, scooting around the corner past* AUGGIE *and* VIOLET *and exiting to the left of frame.*

WOMAN *Thief! Thief! He stole my purse!*
AUGGIE *(Under his breath)* Shit. *(He takes off after the kid—exiting the frame)*

In the meantime, the door behind them opens and a number of customers, attracted by the commotion, come out, crowding around the doorway with the WOMAN and VIOLET. Among them are the three OTB MEN (TOMMY, DENNIS, and JERRY).

WOMAN I can't believe it! He just ripped it out of my hands! Three hundred dollars in cash and all my credit cards!
DENNIS *(Looking the WOMAN up and down)* Yeah, it's disgusting, ain't it? I mean, an attractive lady like yourself, you can't walk the streets of this city alone no more. What you need—
VIOLET *(Excited, looking down the street)* Look! Look! Auggie, he got him!
DENNIS —is a man to protect you.

TOMMY and JERRY both look disgustedly at DENNIS, appalled by his sleazy come-on.

DENNIS (*Playing the innocent. To* TOMMY *and* JERRY) What? What I do now?

TOMMY Give it a rest, Dennis. Can't you see she's upset?

AUGGIE *and the* BOY *reenter frame in front of the door. With one hand,* AUGGIE *is holding him by the collar; in* AUGGIE'S *other hand is the* WOMAN'S *purse. The* BOY *looks terrified.*

AUGGIE (*Handing the* WOMAN *her purse*) Here's your purse.

WOMAN Thank you. That was . . . that was extraordinary. I don't know how to thank you.

AUGGIE Now go inside and call the cops, and we'll have this little punk arrested.

The WOMAN *studies the* BOY, *who stands there in total silence. The others*

watch the exchange between AUGGIE *and the* WOMAN *with rapt attention.*

WOMAN Arrested?
AUGGIE Arrested. He's a thief, ain't he?

The WOMAN *continues to study the* BOY. *Little by little, we see her resolve crumble.*

WOMAN But he's just a baby.
AUGGIE *(Growing irritated)* What difference does it make? He snatched your purse.
WOMAN I have the purse now. Maybe we should just forget it.
AUGGIE Forget it? What are you talking about?
WOMAN He's just a baby. I can't put a baby in jail.
AUGGIE *(By now genuinely angry)* It's your duty! Is this the kind of city you want to live in? Where little kids rip off people's purses—and get away with it?
WOMAN I can't do it. I just can't do it.

AUGGIE *looks at the* WOMAN; *then he looks at the* BOY; *then he looks at the* WOMAN *again. In a flash, he comes to an impulsive, radical decision: he jerks the purse out of the* WOMAN'S *hands and gives it back to the* BOY.

WOMAN *(Shocked)* Hey! What are you doing?
AUGGIE *(To the* BOY, *shooing him away)* Go, kid, go. It's yours.

The BOY, *by now totally confused, stands there mutely with the purse in his hands. He is frozen to the spot.*

WOMAN *(To* AUGGIE, *outraged)* Are you crazy?

The WOMAN *yanks the purse out of the* BOY'S *hands. Without hesitating,* AUGGIE *grabs the purse from the* WOMAN *and gives it back to the* BOY.

AUGGIE *(To the* BOY) Are you deaf? The purse is yours. Now get the fuck out of here! *(He gives the* BOY *a shove, and the* BOY *takes off with the purse, running out of frame)*
WOMAN *(Beside herself)* You son of a bitch! All my money's in there! Are you out of your mind?
AUGGIE *(Boiling over with rage)* No, you are, lady! It's people like you who

are turning New York into such a shit-hole. You won't take responsibility! If we don't teach these kids the difference between right and wrong, who's going to do it?

> This time, the notes were written out in traditional script form. We had a much better idea of what we were looking for now, and the October scenes were devised in an altogether different spirit from the ones we shot in the summer: as a way of filling in gaps, tightening narrative threads, and rounding out the earlier material. The experiment was essentially over, and this time our efforts were concentrated on putting together a viable film.
>
> On the other hand, just because we had a script, that didn't mean the actors weren't free to improvise. The entire cast for this new version of *Philosophers* did an excellent job of playing off and around the material as written, immensely improving it, I feel, with every line they spoke. Mira Sorvino was our principal newcomer, and she fit in as if she had been with us from the beginning. Several things are continually happening at once in this scene, and the side argument between Violet and Auggie as well as Dennis's snickering laugh from the front door help make the action unfold with all the multi-level confusion of a real street scene.

2. INT: NIGHT. VIOLET'S BEDROOM

VIOLET *is sitting alone, putting on her makeup in front of a mirror.*

VIOLET Auggie, you make me so horny. You make my *tripas* . . . tremble. . . . Oh, Auggie, you would be so wonderful . . . if only you were different. *(Pause. She begins opening jars on the table in front of her)* That Auggie, he gonna drive me cuckoo. First he say yes, then he say no. It's on, it's off, it's some other time. But Ramon, he don't know some other time. He play at Freddy's on the sixteenth, and now Agosto, he tell me he busy on the sixteenth. But I tole him: Saturday, the sixteenth. What gives around here, huh? Is somebody deaf or something? I talk myself blue in the face, and still it don't do no good. *(Pause. Fussing with her mascara. Uncaps her lipstick and begins applying it to her lips. Puckers her mouth in the mirror. Growing angrier. As if addressing AUGGIE)* Auggie, I make up my mind. And this is what my mind says. It says: if you don't do the thing you said you would do, then I never say nothing to you no more. You got it? Nothing. Never. No more. *(Pause. Inspects her lips in the mirror. Even angrier: but in a low, quiet, smoldering voice)* You lie to me, Auggie. And people who lie don't deserve no love. You mess with Violetta, and Violetta fight back. (*Almost in a whisper*) I rip your guts out, Auggie. Like a tiger. Like a fucking tiger—with teeth as sharp as the razor blades!

> Violet's monologue is the only interior scene filmed outside the cigar store, but we didn't have far to go: just around the corner to an empty apartment on 16th Street.
> Another departure from the first round of shooting: the close-up. For the first time, we managed to film a scene from two different angles.

3. INT: DAY. THE BROOKLYN CIGAR CO.

AUGGIE *and* VINNIE *are alone in the store, deep in conversation.*

VINNIE I don't know, Auggie. It's a lot of money. I'd be crazy to turn it down.

AUGGIE After nineteen years, you're just going to walk away? I can't believe it.

VINNIE It's dollars and cents. This store's been losing money for years, you know that as well as I do. It's a good month when we break even.

AUGGIE But you've got plenty of money, Vin. All those real estate deals out on the Island. You just write this place off on your taxes.

VINNIE It's too late. We're already in contract.

AUGGIE So the Brooklyn Cigar Company gets turned into a health-food store.

VINNIE Times change. Tobacco's out, wheat germ's in. (*Pause*) It might not be such a bad thing for you either, Auggie. I mean, maybe it's time for you to move on, too. I'd hate to see you turn into an old man sitting behind that counter.

AUGGIE Everybody has to grow old. What difference does it make where it happens?

VINNIE (*Lighting up a cigar. Smiling*) No more free cigars, eh, Auggie?

AUGGIE (*Pensive*) You really should think this through before it's too late, Vincent. I mean, sure, it's just a dinky little nothing store, but everybody comes in here. Not just the smokers . . . but the school kids for their candy . . . old Mrs. McKenna for her soap-opera magazines . . . Crazy Louie for his cough drops . . . Frank Sanchez for his *El Diario* . . . fat Mr. Chen for his crossword-puzzle books. The whole neighborhood lives in this store. It's a

hangout, and it helps hold the place together. Go twenty blocks from here, and twelve-year-old kids are shooting each other for a pair of sneakers. You close this store, and it's one more nail in the coffin. You'll be helping to kill off this neighborhood.

VINNIE You trying to make me feel guilty, is that what you're doing?
AUGGIE No. I'm just giving you the facts. You can do whatever you want with them.

> Victor Argo was performing in a play in Los Angeles and could only work with us on Monday, his day off, which was the last day of our three-day shoot. Harvey Keitel, on the other hand, was only available on the first two days, Thursday and Friday. What to do? How to film a conversation between two men who couldn't be in the same room together? The only possible solution was to cheat. We filmed the two halves of the scene on separate days. Peggy Gormley (Sue from *Cowboys and Indians*) read the lines of the missing actor at each session.

4. INT: DAY. THE BROOKLYN CIGAR CO.

VINNIE *is sitting alone, agitated, still worrying about his recent conversation with* AUGGIE.

VINNIE That Auggie. He's going to drive me crazy. Just when I get the deal together, he comes in and starts playing those fucking violins. Brooklyn, Brooklyn. I'm supposed to care about Brooklyn? I don't even live in this shithole of a town no more.

VINNIE *leans forward, elbows on his knees, and puts his head between his hands. He looks down at the ground. Two beats.*

A figure enters the frame: a large black man dressed in a Brooklyn Dodgers uniform with number 42 on his back. This is JACKIE ROBINSON. *He stops in front of the bench and stares down at* VINNIE. *The rest of the scene plays on* VINNIE'S *face.*

JACKIE ROBINSON Hi, Vinnie. Remember me?
VINNIE *(Awestruck)* Jackie?
JACKIE ROBINSON In the flesh, sport.
VINNIE *(Stammering)* Jackie . . . the greatest player of them all. I used to pray for you at night when I was a kid.
JACKIE ROBINSON I'm the man who changed America, Vinnie. And I did

it right here, in Brooklyn. They spat on me, they cursed me, they made my life a never-ending hell, and I wasn't allowed to fight back. It takes its toll, being a martyr. I died when I was fifty-three, Vinnie, younger than you are now. But I was a hell of a ballplayer, wasn't I?

VINNIE The best. You were the best there was, Jackie.

JACKIE ROBINSON And after me, things started to change. I don't just mean for black people, I mean for white people, too. After me, white people and black people could never look at each other in the same way again. And it all happened right here, sport. In Brooklyn.

VINNIE Yeah. And then they had to move the team away. It nearly broke my heart. *(Pause)* Why'd they have to do a dumb thing like that?

JACKIE ROBINSON Dollars and cents, Vinnie. Ebbets Field might be gone, but what happened there lives on in the mind. That's what counts, Vinnie. Mind over matter. *(We see VINNIE listening intently, making the connection between the fate of the Dodgers and the fate of the cigar store)* And besides, there are more important things in life than baseball. *(Pause. Looking out the window)* But Brooklyn looks good. More or less the way it was when I last saw it. And Prospect Park over there . . . still as beautiful as ever. *(Pause)* Say, Vinnie. They don't still make those Belgian waffles, do they? Man, what I wouldn't give to sink my teeth into a Belgian waffle. With two scoops of pistachio ice cream on it . . . and maybe a heap of strawberries and bananas on top of that. Boy, have I missed those things.

VINNIE *(Obligingly)* Belgian waffles? Sure, they still make them. *(Points)* A couple of blocks down, you'll see the Cosmic Diner. Just go in there, and they'll give you all the Belgian waffles you want.

JACKIE ROBINSON Thanks, sport. Don't mind if I do. *(Begins to exit frame. Stops)* A day in Brooklyn just wouldn't be complete without stopping in for a Belgian waffle, would it? *(He exits frame)*

Still sitting on the chair, VINNIE follows JACKIE ROBINSON with his eyes. After a moment, he turns back and looks straight into the camera. His expression is utterly blank. Hold for two beats.

This scene was written two or three days after the rest of the October material, and the idea came directly from Harvey Weinstein, president of Miramax.

It was 10:00 P.M. when the telephone rang at my house. Harvey was on the other end of the line, calling from his hotel room in London, where it was three o'clock in the morning. He had just had a dream about *Blue in the Face*, he said, and he wondered if it wouldn't make sense to work it into the film: after his conversation with Auggie about selling the store, Vinnie is miserable and confused; he sits down somewhere to weigh the pros and cons of his dilemma, when all of a sudden, out of thin air, a number of the old Dodgers appear to him and begin reminiscing about Brooklyn. What did I think? I thought it was a stroke of genius. First thing tomorrow morning, I would sit down at my desk and see what I could do.

One of the Dodgers Harvey mentioned was Jackie Robinson. He couldn't have known, of course, but I had been thinking about Jackie Robinson all my life. Way back when I was in the ninth grade, everyone in my junior high school was required to participate in a public speaking contest. The subject that year was "The Person I Most Admire." I wrote my speech about Jackie Robinson and wound up winning the first prize. It was 1961, and I was just fourteen years old, but composing that speech was one of the crucial events of my life. After that day, I knew that I wanted to become a writer.

When I sat down to work on the scene, I realized that Jackie Robinson was the only Dodger who had to appear, that his presence would say everything that had to be said. . . .

5. EXT: DAY. IN FRONT OF THE BROOKLYN CIGAR CO.

AUGGIE *is standing in front of the door, smoking a cigarette and surveying the street.*

A YOUNG WOMAN *dressed in a skimpy Las Vegas showgirl outfit and wearing a little bellhop's cap on her head approaches the store. She is holding a yellow envelope in her hand.* AUGGIE *studies her with a mixture of amusement and curiosity.*

YOUNG WOMAN Is this the Brooklyn Cigar Company?
AUGGIE In the flesh. What can I do for you?
YOUNG WOMAN (*Studying the envelope*) I'm looking for Mr. Augustus Wren.
AUGGIE You've found him, beautiful.
YOUNG WOMAN (*Relieved*) Great. I've never been to Brooklyn before. I wasn't sure I'd be able to find you.
AUGGIE Well, Brooklyn's on the map. We even have streets out here. And electricity, too.
YOUNG WOMAN (*Sarcastic*) You don't say. (*Pause*) Well?
AUGGIE Well what?

YOUNG WOMAN I have a telegram for you.

AUGGIE Nobody's dead, I hope. *(Extending his hand)* Let's see it.

YOUNG WOMAN A singing telegram.

AUGGIE *(Grinning)* This gets better and better.

YOUNG WOMAN *(Gearing up for her performance)* Ready?

AUGGIE Whenever you are.

YOUNG WOMAN *(Dancing as she sings. In a throaty, nightclub singer's voice)*

> The deal is off . . . stop.
> Ba-ba-ba-ba-ba-boom.
> Not selling the store . . . stop.
> Ba-ba-ba-ba-ba-boom.
> See you next week . . . stop.
> Ba-ba-ba-ba-ba-boom.
> I'm sending you love . . . love . . . love
> From Las Vegas!
> Ba-ba-ba-ba-ba-boom.

AUGGIE *(Claps in appreciation)* Dynamite.

The YOUNG WOMAN gives a polite curtsy (in stark contrast to her raunchy performance) and smiles.

AUGGIE (cont'd) I'd say that's worth at least a five-dollar tip, wouldn't you? *(Removes his wallet from his pocket)*

YOUNG WOMAN *(Quietly miffed by the small amount)* Five dollars?

AUGGIE *hands her a five-dollar bill; she gives him the yellow envelope.*

AUGGIE Any time you want to deliver some more good news, you know where to find me.

YOUNG WOMAN *(Looking at the money)* Thanks, mister. Now I'll be able to buy that hearing aid my mother's always wanted.

The YOUNG WOMAN *walks off.* AUGGIE *opens the envelope and begins reading the telegram, humming under his breath: Ba-ba-ba-ba-ba-boom.*

> This was the first time I had ever written anything to be sung. Admittedly, the lyrics of the telegram message aren't much to write home about, but still, I had a definite melody in mind when I wrote the words. To my amazement, Madonna sang it precisely as I imagined she would. Beat for beat, phrase

for phrase, she delivered the same little tune I had been carrying around in my head. The only difference: there were five ba's before each of my booms, and she used seven.

6. EXT: DAY. IN FRONT OF THE BROOKLYN CIGAR CO.

AUGGIE *is sitting outside the store in his plastic lawn chair, reading* The Philosophical Investigations *by Ludwig Wittgenstein and smoking two cigarettes at once. A boom box sits at his feet.*

VIOLET *comes by in a tight dress and stops in front of AUGGIE'S chair.*

VIOLET I just wanted to show you what I'm wearing tonight. *(She spins in a circle, modeling her dress)* So you'll know what you'll be missing if you don't do the thing you said you'd do.
AUGGIE *(Admiringly)* Very nice.
VIOLET *(Noticing that AUGGIE has two cigarettes in his mouth)* Auggie, you got two cigarettes in your mouth. What do you want to do a thing like that for?
AUGGIE *(Shrugs)* I don't know. It seemed like a good idea at the time. *(Pause)* You want one?

VIOLET *shrugs.* AUGGIE *takes one of the cigarettes out of his mouth and hands it to her.*

VIOLET *(Smoking)* So, what are *you* going to wear tonight, Auggie?
AUGGIE *(Shrugs)* I don't know. I haven't thought about it yet.
VIOLET I hope you'll be ready, that's all I can say. *(Gesturing to her body)* It would be sad to say good-bye to this, wouldn't it, Auggie?
AUGGIE What do you mean? I'm ready now.
VIOLET You're not even dressed. How can you be ready?
AUGGIE I might not be dressed. But I'm ready.
VIOLET What the hell does that mean?
AUGGIE Watch.

AUGGIE *pushes a button on the boom box. Loud salsa music suddenly comes pouring out of the machine.* AUGGIE *stands up and invites* VIOLET *to dance.*

The camera begins to pull away. VIOLET *throws her head back and laughs, then starts dancing in front of* AUGGIE. *After a few moments, other people enter the frame, all of them dancing to the music. Cut to:*

The street from above. Dozens of people have appeared out of nowhere. A wild block party is in full swing. AUGGIE *and* VIOLET *continue to dance, laughing in the midst of the mayhem.*

> For reasons still difficult to understand, the first part of this scene did not play well on screen. The performances were good, but the light, perhaps, or the camera angle, or the quality of the sound just didn't work, and we reluctantly dropped it from the film.
> The two block-party shots, however, still provide us with our conclusion. The tall blonde dancing in the middle of the crowd is RuPaul.

7. Statistics

One by one, different people stand in front of the cigar store and recite the following facts about Brooklyn:

—There are 2.3 million people living in Brooklyn.
—There are 1,600 miles of streets, 4,513 fire boxes, and 50 miles of shoreline in Brooklyn.
—There are 672,569 people living in Brooklyn who were born in foreign countries.
—There are 3,268,121 potholes in Brooklyn.
—There are 605,554 people under the age of 18 living in Brooklyn.
—There were 1,066 forcible rapes committed in Brooklyn last year.
—There are 872,305 African Americans living in Brooklyn.
—There are 412,906 Jewish people living in Brooklyn.
—There are 462,411 Hispanic people living in Brooklyn.
—There are 514,163 people living below the poverty line in Brooklyn.
—There were 32,979 cars stolen in Brooklyn last year.
—There are 90 different ethnic groups, 32,000 businesses, and 1,500 churches, synagogues, and mosques in Brooklyn.
—There were 30,973 robberies, 14,596 felonious assaults, and 720 murders committed in Brooklyn last year.
—Every day, 7,999 Belgian waffles are eaten in the restaurants of Brooklyn.
—Once, there was a major league baseball team in Brooklyn. But that was a long time ago.

In editing the July material (before we knew we would have a chance to shoot again in October) I suggested a number of small elements that could be added to the film without major expense. The map of Brooklyn that appears at the beginning (along with the words "YOU ARE HERE") was one such idea. Another was to flash various facts and statistics about Brooklyn on screen at certain key moments. Once the extra days of shooting were given to us, we decided it would be more interesting to have a cross-section of Auggie's customers recite those figures on the sidewalk outside the store. A casting session was hastily arranged, and more than a hundred people showed up to audition for these briefest of brief roles. (Among them was Michelle Hurst, who had played Rashid's Aunt Em in *Smoke*.) A video tape was sent to me, and in less than two hours I chose a dozen people to play our Brooklyn "statisticians." A perfect example of the deadlines and pressures we had to deal with in setting up our second round of shooting.

8. Violet Singing "Fever"

After the first round of shooting in July, Miramax threw a small cast party at Sammy's Rumanian Restaurant on the Lower East Side. The highlight of the evening came when Mel Gorham stood up on the little stage and sang an unforgettable rendition of "Fever." Wayne, who was still fighting the bug in his system, had left the party by then and missed the performance. Just one or two days before we began shooting again, he said to me, "Everyone is still talking about how great Mel was when she sang 'Fever.' Why don't we have her do it for us after she finishes her monologue?" "Why not?" I said. And so we hired a couple of musicians to accompany Mel, and Wayne finally got to see her do the number—in a radically different version.

Later on, when we were putting together the final cut of the film, we brought Mel back to loop the lines she speaks over the song.

9. Belgian Waffle Poster

The Waffle Man carries around a Belgian waffle menu that features a succulent, full-color photo of his heart's desire. When we filmed Lily Tomlin's scene in July, there was no time to do an insert shot of the photo, which would have given the audience a clear idea of what her character so desperately craved. To remedy this lack, we prepared a shot of a Belgian waffle poster in October—which turned out to be the last shot of the film. . . .

The poster was taped to a wall inside the cigar store. We planned the shot to last a certain number of seconds (I forget how many), and then the camera started to roll. With just two or three seconds left, the tape suddenly loosened and the poster fell off the wall. It was a typical *Blue in the Face* moment. We thought we were finished, but the god of adhesives had decided to play one last prank on us. So the poster had to be remounted, and the shot had to be done again.

This time it worked. This time the movie was really over.

10. Video Material

This was the final piece of the puzzle. In discussing ways to open up *Blue in the Face,* Wayne and I became attracted to the idea of going out into Brooklyn and talking to real people, of pushing certain parts of our film into the realm of pure documentary. Yes, the cigar store was an imaginary place peopled by imaginary characters, but so much vital energy had come from the actors' performances that it didn't feel like a contradiction to try to include the actual Brooklyn world that surrounds the store . . . and see what happened when we mixed the two elements.

In an effort to save both time and money, Wayne suggested that we shoot these documentary sequences in High-8 video and then, once we were in the cutting room, transfer the material we wanted to keep onto film. Since we would be too busy on the set to take care of it ourselves, we had to enlist

someone else's help. That person turned out to be photographer Harvey Wang, author of *Harvey Wang's New York.*

Given that both our leading actor and producer were named Harvey, and given that Wayne's last name was Wang, it felt like some kind of weird, cosmic joke that the best man for the job should be named Harvey Wang. To enhance the beauty of the coincidence, Harvey Wang is not Chinese (as Wayne is) but Jewish (as Wayne's co-director is). So, a Chinese Jewish team making a film about Brooklyn brought in a Jewish man with a Chinese name who just happened to live in Brooklyn. What could be more appropriate? The three of us laughed about it constantly, and Wayne never tired of introducing Harvey to other people as his brother. But underneath all the horseplay, there was something wonderfully in keeping with the spirit of the project we had undertaken. This was *Blue in the Face* in a nutshell: strange, unpredictable doings set against a backdrop of diversity, tolerance, and affection.

Harvey threw himself into his assignment with great relish. In eight days of work, he amassed over sixteen hours of footage. No more than a few minutes are included in *Blue in the Face,* but having seen every one of the several dozen interviews he recorded, I believe this material would make an excellent film in its own right: a documentary portrait of Brooklyn in all its rough-and-tumble glory. As Harvey himself has written: "There is no one voice for all of Brooklyn. Like an orchestra, each voice contributes an accent, a 'fuck you buddy, that's my parking space' attitude, a cheer, a kvetch. The resulting cacophony is the soundtrack of this one-of-a-kind place."

It's all there in his film.

blue in the face

Situations created by **Paul Auster and Wayne Wang**
Directed by **Wayne Wang and Paul Auster**
Produced by **Greg Johnson, Peter Newman,**
and Diana Phillips
Director of Photography: **Adam Holender**
Editor: **Christopher Tellefsen**
Production Designer: **Kalina Ivanov**
Costumes: **Claudia Brown**
Executive Producers: **Harvey Keitel, Bob Weinstein,**
and Harvey Weinstein,
Still Photographers: **Barry Wetcher and K.C. Baily**

Cast
(in order of appearance)
Man with Unusual Glasses **Lou Reed**
Auggie Wren **Harvey Keitel**
Violet **Mel Gorham**
Boy **Sharif Rashed**
Young Woman **Mira Sorvino**
Jerry **José Zuniga**
Dennis **Steve Gevedon**
Vinnie **Victor Argo**
Sue **Peggy Gormley**
Jimmy Rose **Jared Harris**
Tommy **Giancarlo Esposito**
Dot **Roseanne**
Bob **Jim Jarmusch**
Waffle Man **Lily Tomlin**
Rapper **Malik Yoba**
Pete **Michael J. Fox**
Jackie Robinson **Keith David**
Messenger **Madonna**
Musicians **John Lurie, Billy Martin, Calvin Weston**
Dancer **RuPaul**

Brooklyn Residents **Rusty Kanokogi**

Sasalina Gambino

Cheif Bey

Ian Frazier

Luc Sante

Robert Jackson

1. INT: DAY. THE BROOKLYN CIGAR CO.

A MAN WITH UNUSUAL GLASSES *sits behind the counter.*

MAN

I think one of the reasons I live in New York is because . . . I know my way around New York. I don't know my way around Paris. I don't know my way around Denver. I don't know my way around Maui. I don't know my way around Toronto, et cetera and so on. It's almost by default. I don't know very many people who live in New York who don't also say,

"But I'm leaving." I've been thinking of leaving for . . . thirty-five years now. I'm almost ready.

2. MAPS

We see a map of the northeastern section of the United States. The camera moves in on New York. A second map appears of New York City. The camera moves in on the Brooklyn streets. When we reach the corner of 16th Street and Prospect Park West, a circle is drawn around the spot. Words are written out across the screen: "YOU ARE HERE."

EXT: DAY. THE BROOKLYN CIGAR CO.

Establishing shot of the cigar shop across the street. Closer shot: we see various customers going in and out the front door.

4. EXT: DAY. THE CORNER IN FRONT OF THE BROOKLYN CIGAR CO.

AUGGIE and VIOLET *are standing together on the corner.*

                    VIOLET
Saturday the sixteenth.

                    AUGGIE
(Imitating VIOLET'S accent) Saturday the sixteenth.

                    VIOLET
Yes.

                    AUGGIE
(Correcting her pronunciation) Saturday the sixteenth.

                    VIOLET
Saturday the sixteenth. It has to be that night. It's got to be because that's

the only night Ramon and his band are playing in Brooklyn. Okay? Auggie, he's my brother. Trust me, okay?

> AUGGIE

Don't worry, sweetheart. It's a date. *(He kisses her)*

> VIOLET

Thank you. Listen, you're going to be so special. Just remember the steps I teach you, and you're going to be like Fred fucking Astaire.

> AUGGIE

Okay, Ginger. Whatever you say.

In the background, we see a BOY snatch a YOUNG WOMAN'S purse. He scoots around the corner past AUGGIE and VIOLET and exits frame.

> YOUNG WOMAN

Thief! Thief! He took my purse!

AUGGIE chases after the BOY. A moment later he drags him back, holding him by the collar. He hands the YOUNG WOMAN her purse.

> YOUNG WOMAN

(To AUGGIE) Thank you. Thank you very much, sir.

> AUGGIE

Are you okay?

> YOUNG WOMAN

I really appreciate it. Thank you. That was great.

> AUGGIE

Okay, all right. Good. *(Looks at BOY)* All right, let's go call the cops. Get this little kid arrested.

> YOUNG WOMAN

Wait a second here.

> AUGGIE

We'll call from inside the store.

YOUNG WOMAN

You're going to have him arrested?

AUGGIE

Yeah.

The YOUNG WOMAN *leans over and studies the* BOY *closely.*

AUGGIE

No, no! Don't!

YOUNG WOMAN

(To BOY) How old are you?

AUGGIE

I see it in your eyes. *(Imitating a little boy's voice)* "Me? I'm only twelve."
Is that what you're going to give me now, lady?

YOUNG WOMAN

He's scared to death. Come on.

AUGGIE

I'm scared to death of *him. (Again, imitating a little boy's voice)* "I'm only
twelve years old . . . "

YOUNG WOMAN

You caught him in about five seconds flat . . .

AUGGIE

" . . . I only shoot people who can't catch me, who are too old."

YOUNG WOMAN

Mister, come on. Listen, I thank you for getting it back, but let him go.
He's too little.

VIOLET

(Trying to put an end to the dispute) Okay. All right.

AUGGIE

You're not going to press charges against him? You're not going to press
charges?

YOUNG WOMAN

No. Look at him. He's a baby.

AUGGIE

Look at him. What about him?

YOUNG WOMAN

He looks like my little brother.

AUGGIE

Sweetheart, babies are shooting people in New York today.

YOUNG WOMAN

Do you see a gun on him? Come on.

AUGGIE

Do you read the papers?

AUGGIE

(To BOY) You got a gun on you? (Begins searching him)

YOUNG WOMAN

Come on. You're kidding me. Let him go, all right? Come on. The joke's over.

VIOLET

(To AUGGIE). Come on, stop it.

YOUNG WOMAN

Leave him alone, please.

JERRY

Just call the cops.

YOUNG WOMAN

Just let him go, all right? I don't care. I don't want to press charges. Thank you. I do appreciate you getting the purse back, but please let him go. He's going to be good. Look at him . . . (TO BOY) You're not going to do anything anymore.

AUGGIE takes the purse from the YOUNG WOMAN and hands it to the BOY.

AUGGIE

(To BOY) Here, it's yours.

YOUNG WOMAN

What? Oh, come on. *(She takes the purse back from the BOY)*

VIOLET

(To AUGGIE) I want you to know, you're looking for trouble here. You're looking for trouble.

Once again, AUGGIE takes the purse from the YOUNG WOMAN and hands it to the BOY. This time he gives him a shove.

AUGGIE

(To BOY) Go! Go!

The BOY runs off. A moment later, the YOUNG WOMAN exits, running after the BOY.

VIOLET

(To AUGGIE) Why you do that? You shit! Look at the poor girl. Why you do that? You fuck! *(Turning to the onlookers)* Why you stand there? Do something! You think it's funny?

The YOUNG WOMAN returns empty-handed.

YOUNG WOMAN

(To AUGGIE) How dare you do that! How dare you take my thing and give it away like that! Do you know what is in there?

DENNIS *begins to snicker.*

YOUNG WOMAN

(To DENNIS) Shut up!

DENNIS *goes into the store, still laughing.*

AUGGIE

Lady, lady . . .

YOUNG WOMAN

What? What are you doing?

AUGGIE

If that bag was so important to you, then you should hang on to it.

YOUNG WOMAN

What are you, some kind of vigilante?

AUGGIE

I put my life at risk to catch that kid.

YOUNG WOMAN

Well thank you very much. But I have a right to forgive somebody and not be punished for it.

VIOLET

Okay. . . .

AUGGIE

You've got a responsib. . . (To VIOLET) Excuse me, sweetheart. Give me a minute. Give me a minute!

VIOLET

Don't talk to me like that, Auggie.

AUGGIE turns back to the WOMAN, wagging his finger in her face.

AUGGIE

You've got a responsibility to teach that kid right. . . .

YOUNG WOMAN

(Brushing away AUGGIE'S hand) Don't stick that finger in my face. You have no right!

AUGGIE

No, lady. Lady. . . .

YOUNG WOMAN

Oh, lady, lady, lady! What is this?

AUGGIE

You've got a responsibility to teach this kid right from wrong.

YOUNG WOMAN

I . . . Oh? And you just taught him right from wrong? That was right from wrong? What you just did was reward him!

AUGGIE

You know what you taught him? (Pause. Astonished) I rewarded him? (Turns and looks to the sky. Gesturing) Mama! Oh God! Please!

YOUNG WOMAN

You gave it back to him! Stop it!

AUGGIE

(Incredulous) I rewarded him?

YOUNG WOMAN

You just gave it back. What was that? It was an encouragement! Mine was a lesson of clemency!

AUGGIE

Clemency?

YOUNG WOMAN

I showed him a little bit of kindness.

AUGGIE

Lady! (Shouting) This is New York!

5. INT: DAY. THE BROOKLYN CIGAR CO.

The MAN WITH UNUSUAL GLASSES, as before.

MAN

I'm scared in my own apartment. I'm scared twenty-four hours a day. But not necessarily in New York. I actually feel pretty comfortable in New York. I get scared . . . like in Sweden. You know, it's kind of empty.

They're all drunk. Everything works. If you stop at a stop light and don't turn your engine off, people come over and talk to you about it. You go to the medicine cabinet and open it up, and there'll be a little poster saying, "In case of suicide, call . . . " You turn on the TV, there's an ear operation. These things scare me. New York? No.

6. EXT: DAY. IN FRONT OF THE BROOKLYN CIGAR CO.

One by one, three people recite the following statistics:

FIRST WOMAN
There are 2.3 million people living in Brooklyn.

OLD MAN
There are 90 different ethnic groups, 32,000 businesses, and 1,500 churches, synagogues, and mosques in Brooklyn.

SECOND WOMAN
There were 30,973 robberies, 14,596 felonious assaults, and 720 murders committed in Brooklyn last year.

7. INT: DAY. THE BROOKLYN CIGAR CO.

AUGGIE and VINNIE are alone in the store. We catch them in mid-conversation.

AUGGIE
No problem, Vin. Everything's under control. I could run this store in my sleep.

VINNIE
I know. How long you been working for me, Auggie?

AUGGIE
I don't know. Thirteen, fourteen years. Something like that.

VINNIE

It's kind of crazy, don't you think? I mean, a smart guy like you. What do you want to hold on to a dead-end job like this for?

AUGGIE

I don't know. Maybe because I love you so much, boss.

VINNIE *moves next to AUGGIE and puts his arm around him.*

VINNIE

I love you, too.

AUGGIE *backs off, making a sign of the cross to keep VINNIE at a distance.*

8. EXT: DAY. THE BROOKLYN BRIDGE

A car travels across the bridge toward Brooklyn. Shot in video.

9. CARD

Words appear on screen: "Brooklyn Attitude."

10. BROOKLYN RESIDENT INTERVIEW

Shot in video. Apartment interior.

RUSTY KANOKOGI

(With her husband beside her) The Brooklyn attitude, as far as I'm concerned, is first, knowing what you're doing, being right, and following through. And never stop following through on what you believe in. And if you have to defend it—physically, verbally, spiritually, whatever way you have to defend it. Brooklyn people are always ready to pay the price for what they believe in. It's being up front and following through. And not taking any crap from anybody.

11. INT: DAY. THE BROOKLYN CIGAR CO.

AUGGIE *is behind the counter.* SUE, *a waitress, is putting coins down in front of him.* JIMMY *is dusting the wooden Indian.* TOMMY, JERRY, *and* DENNIS *are sitting in chairs along the side window.*

> SUE

A pack of Kools, please.

> DENNIS

(Muttering) What's she doing in here?

> SUE

I heard you, Dennis.

> DENNIS

Huh?

> SUE

I heard you, Dennis. This is a public place.

> DENNIS

Yeah, it's a public place, whatever. *(Sarcastically)* How're you doing, Sue?

> SUE

(Walking over to face DENNIS. With equal sarcasm) How're you doing, Dennis?

> DENNIS

Oh, I'm good. I'm always good.

> SUE

Well, I'm glad to see your fingers aren't broken.

> DENNIS

What the . . . ? What's that supposed to mean?

> SUE

Well, if your fingers were broken, at least you'd have an excuse for not calling Mary last night. She sat by the phone all night. She thought that something had happened. Oh, maybe Dennis . . . maybe something happened. Fool. If you tell her you're going to meet her, you come. Or at least you call.

                              DENNIS

What?

                               SUE

Oh Dennis, don't act like that. Don't act like you don't know what I'm talking about.

                              DENNIS

No, wait, wait. Wait, wait, wait, wait . . . What are you coming in here telling me. . . ?

                               SUE

I was hoping I'd bump into you.

                              DENNIS

Wait. What are you coming in here telling me . . . no, let me fin— What are you coming in here telling me what to do with my girlfriend?

                               SUE

Your girlfriend?

                              DENNIS

I think . . .

                               SUE

If you cared an ounce about Mary, you would not let her sit there all night waiting for you.

                              DENNIS

Mary and I have an understanding. See, I work for a living. *(Talking over her)* I don't know what you do. Well, I know what you do. You spend ten hours a day standing around a diner making twenty-five. . . . I work for a living. I have a schedule. I have people . . .

                               SUE

A schedule?

DENNIS

A very . . .

SUE

The Knick game's at eight o'clock. That means at seven o'clock you're out there with the tickets. That's a schedule?

DENNIS

It's a schedule. It's a job. It's where I have to be. It's something that she understands. Okay? *(Continuing to talk over her)* Now what are you doing? I don't know, what are you doing here even like deciding what she needs to think I need? What are you getting in my shit for?

SUE

I don't give a shit what you do with your life. Do whatever you want.

DENNIS

Well, then, shut up about it.

SUE

Then leave my sister in peace.

DENNIS

Then shut up about it! Then shut up about it! Why do you come in here? This place . . .

DENNIS *turns and gestures toward the others.* SUE *touches him lightly on the back.*

SUE

I don't like to see my sister . . .

DENNIS

(Wheeling around) Don't touch me! How about you don't touch me at all. Okay? How about you keep your greasy little diner fucking fingers off me? All right?

SUE

What?

DENNIS

You know, you know I . . . *(Addressing the others in the store)*

SUE

Where do you come off?

DENNIS

I spent a year listening to Phil. My good friend, you know Phil . . . I spent a fucking year listening to him bitch about you. A year! And now you're going to tell me how to run my relationship? You're going to tell me what I should do to my girlfriend . . . or what I shouldn't do?

SUE

I'm just asking. . . .

DENNIS

I believe Phil left you. I think that was the case, right? I think he left you, if I'm not mistaken about that.

SUE

I don't think that was the sequence of events. . . .

DENNIS

(Talking over her) He left you because . . . Well, I think . . . Well, no. What was it then? What? You left him? No, I don't think so. I don't think so. No, he left you. *(Turning to the others)* You know why? You know why he left her? Frigid.

SUE

I'm glad you're an expert. . . .

DENNIS

Frigid. That's why. Frigid. Nothing. Nothing, nothing, nothing. Ice bitch.

SUE

Fuck you!

DENNIS

Ice bitch!

SUE *slaps* DENNIS *in the face.*

                                    SUE
Fuck you! You bastard!

12. BROOKLYN RESIDENT INTERVIEW

Shot in video. Continues from Scene 10.

                          RUSTY KANOKOGI
I taught him handball. And he's my best opponent. Because the score is
always tied. We don't fight at home because we fight on the court. And
I'm talking about drop-dead fights. I won't give, I'll die, I'll fall down on
that court before I'll give him a point. And then he tries to harass me, you
know? "Oh," he says, "now I'm going to get serious." And every time he
does that, I kick his butt.

13. INT: DAY. THE BROOKLYN CIGAR CO.

Continues from Scene 11.

                               DENNIS
(In a rage) What the fuck you come in here doing this shit for? These are
my friends!

                               TOMMY
(Trying to calm him) Dennis.

                               DENNIS
(Addressing SUE, pointing to AUGGIE) You're telling him how to run his
business? These are my friends! What the hell you come in here for and
tell my friends . . .

                               TOMMY
Dennis, come on.

                              DENNIS
No! Fuck you! Fuck you, fuck you, fuck you!

                              TOMMY
All right, all right, go on out of here. Just go outside. Forget about it, just
forget about it.

DENNIS *storms out. Dissolve.* JIMMY ROSE *is standing next to* SUE *in front
of the counter.*

                              JIMMY
What were you yelling about?

                               SUE
(To AUGGIE*)* Is that what this is about? You guys sit around here and talk
this trash all day?

                             AUGGIE
No, Sue, no.

                               SUE
I'm sorry I started it. Believe me, I know I started it.

                             AUGGIE
Nobody talks about you.

                              JIMMY
What . . . what were you yelling about?

                               SUE
(To JIMMY*)* Things we shouldn't have been yelling about.

                              JIMMY
You want a hug?

                               SUE
Yeah.

                              JIMMY
Yeah?

                              2 1 8

JIMMY *gives* SUE *a tentative embrace and pats her on the shoulder. Then he hugs her more tightly, leaning his head against her chest. She laughs.*

                              SUE
Get right in there, Jimmy.

                              JIMMY
Do you feel better?

                              SUE
Yeah, a lot better.

                              JIMMY
You're not rigid anymore?

                              SUE
No, no, not rigid.

                              JIMMY
Yeah, I get rigid sometimes. Yeah. *(He turns and points to the wooden Indian)* Like the Indian over there.

                              SUE
Yeah?

                              JIMMY
Yeah. I . . . I stand over there and get rigid.

14. INT: DAY. THE BROOKLYN CIGAR CO.

JIMMY ROSE *is sitting on a stool in front of the counter.*

                              JIMMY
Auggie says that . . . he says that . . . first of all, you, he says first of all you like somebody . . . and . . . and then . . . then you kiss them. And then after you kiss them, uhhh . . . you do the dirty. Yeah. Yeah. Doing the dirty. Yeah. He says . . . and after that . . . uhhh . . . then you find out if uhhh . . . if you can fall in love with them. And if you fall in love with them, you marry somebody else.

15. INT: DAY. THE BROOKLYN CIGAR CO.

JIMMY ROSE *is dusting the wooden Indian.* AUGGIE *is doing inventory.*
DOT *enters.*

> DOT

(To JIMMY*)* Hey.

> JIMMY

Hey.

> DOT

(To AUGGIE*)* Hi.

> AUGGIE

Hi, Dot. How are you, kid?

> DOT

Well, I'm just great. I'm just great. Can I have gum? *(She takes a pack
from the shelf)* I'm just real fucking great.

> AUGGIE

What brings you to sunny Brooklyn?

> DOT

I just drove in. I wanted to talk to you. If I can talk to you? Can I talk to
you? Do you have a minute?

> AUGGIE

You caught me at a bad time. I'm taking inventory.

> DOT

Oh, a minute. A minute!

> AUGGIE

All right.

> DOT

I'm so fucking pissed off! Goddamn it, I'm so fucking pissed off at Vinnie.
(She sits down in a chair) I just wanted to talk to you about it. I don't

know why I want to talk to you about it, but you know him. I don't know.
I don't know him.

AUGGIE

What happened?

DOT

He just drives me out of my fucking mind. You know what I mean? He
promised that he was going to take me to Las Vegas. You heard about
that and everything. And then, at the last minute, of course, "Another
time." He pulls out and says we'll postpone it, or cancel it, or whatever
the fuck he said. Well, I don't know, but I'm not going. He's not going
with me anyway.

AUGGIE

Yeah?

DOT

And I'm mad, because I was really looking forward to it, and I really
wanted to go, and I've been wanting to go my whole life. But instead of
being able to go there, what did I do? I just sat there washing dishes and
making tuna fish casseroles *for fifteen years!* And I don't get to go to Las

Vegas. And I'm pissed, and I can't get on this chair. Shit!

AUGGIE

Well, Dot, he must have had a good reason for cancelling. . . .

DOT

He doesn't have a good reason. There is no good reason. I mean, there's a million reasons, but none of them are good. You tell your wife of fifteen years that you're going to take her someplace, there's no goddamn good reason to cancel it or postpone it or put it off or nothing. *(Jumpcut)* I wanted to have some excitement. I wanted to go where there's things happening at night. After six.

AUGGIE

How about your bed?

DOT

(Laughs) Like I said, that's why I want to go to Las Vegas. . . .

AUGGIE

Come on.

DOT

Come on? You don't know. You don't know.

AUGGIE

Aw, Vinnie's a wonderful guy. Come on, he loves you, he's crazy about the kids. So the guy, at one time, he broke a promise.

DOT

It isn't one time, it's every time. It's fifteen years' worth of times. It's not one time! If it was one time, do you think I'd be this upset? If it was one time, I'd be like, "That's okay, that's okay, Vinnie." But it's . . . it's always! It's always, unless it has something to do with you . . . or this store.

AUGGIE

Jesus, Dot.

DOT

I never do anything fun. I'm a fun girl!

Cut briefly to musicians playing on the sidewalk outside the store. Then cut back inside.

> DOT

Can I really talk to you?

> AUGGIE

Of course, Dot, of course.

The front door opens and VIOLET enters.

> DOT

Auggie, he just . . . I don't know. . . .

> AUGGIE

Hey, Violet, how are you?

> VIOLET

Hi, Dot.

> DOT

Hi.

> AUGGIE

You know Dot. Dot, Violet.

> DOT

Yeah, hi, Violet.

> VIOLET

Hi, Dot.

> AUGGIE

What's doing, baby?

> VIOLET

Well, I come . . . let me make it a little clearer . . . I come to tell you this Saturday night, you and me, chickie-chickie, dancie-dancie, remember, okay?

You're going dancing, huh? Well, don't cancel. *(She stands up)* I'll see you later.

AUGGIE

Okay, listen. . . .

DOT

Yeah. Don't cancel, though. *(To VIOLET)* Don't let him cancel.

AUGGIE

We don't cancel.

VIOLET

He don't cancel with me.

AUGGIE

Vinnie doesn't cancel either. Vinnie doesn't cancel. . . .

DOT

Don't give me your shit. I'll see you later.

AUGGIE

All right. Be good. *(He pats her on the behind as she leaves. Then, turning to VIOLET)* How are you doing, gorgeous?

VIOLET

Oh, how are you? Nice to see you, baby. *(She kisses AUGGIE on the cheek)* So you and I, we go dancie-dancie, okay? Saturday night.

AUGGIE

Saturday night?

VIOLET

Yeah.

AUGGIE

Not this Saturday night. You mean the Saturday night after.

Bullshit, Auggie. Bullshit.

VIOLET *stamps her cigarette out on the floor.*

AUGGIE

Oh! What are you doing?

VIOLET

What are you doing to me?

AUGGIE

(Pointing to JIMMY) Don't do that. He's got to sweep up the floor. *(AUGGIE picks up the bull)*

VIOLET

Auggie, you said Saturday night. Don't bullshit me, okay? What kind of number you trying to pull on me? You say the sixteenth, we say the sixteenth, I planned the whole night.

AUGGIE

Jesus, is something in the air? What's the matter with you? Dottie's upset, you're upset. About what? *(Pause)* What's in your ear?

VIOLET

(Gesturing to small earphone) It's my music.

AUGGIE

Listen sweetheart, Saturday night . . . Saturday night I promised Tommy I'd clean out his brother's apartment with him. You know, his brother . . . his brother Chuck. We were in the navy together, and he died. You know what I'm saying?

VIOLET

I don't know what you're talking about, okay? Chuck, Chuck. Who the fuck is Chuck?

AUGGIE

No, who the fuck *was* Chuck. Chuck is dead. Chuck's a guy I was in the navy with, and he died.

VIOLET

You're two-timing me, ain't you, baby? Come here.

VIOLET *sidles up to* AUGGIE *and embraces him.*

AUGGIE

Two-timing you? You're too beautiful to two-time.

VIOLET

Who is it? Dot? Sally? Oh, I know . . . it's the little waitress with the big fat *culo*, isn't it?

AUGGIE

You give me more credit than I deserve, doll. No, no, I would never two-time you. What's the matter with you? I love you. Come on, stop. *(He puts his arms around her)*

16. EXT: DAY. IN FRONT OF THE BROOKLYN CIGAR CO.

AUGGIE *walks outside, lights a cigarette, and scans the street.*

17. INT: NIGHT. VIOLET'S BEDROOM

VIOLET *is sitting at her dressing table, looking into the mirror and putting on her makeup.*

VIOLET

(In tears) You lie to me, Agosto. And people who lie don't deserve no love. You mess with Violetta, and Violetta fight back. I rip your guts out, Auggie. Like a tiger. Like a fucking tiger . . . with teeth as sharp as the razor blades. *(Takes a drag of her cigarette)* Don't fuck with me.

18. BROOKLYN RESIDENT INTERVIEW

Shot in video. The boardwalk at Coney Island.

SASALINA GAMBINO

Is a Brooklyn girl a good fighter? Of course. Because we don't scratch and pull hair. We fight like guys. Fist to fist, you know what I'm saying? If we can't beat the other girl, we'll use a garbage can . . . or a bottle . . . or anything. *(Jumpcut)* Do I have a boyfriend? Yeah. He's a roughneck, though. He's not like me. He don't like looking at stuff and chilling out. He just wants to go smoke weed and drink forties all day. And that's all he does. I mean, I think he smokes a pound of weed a day. *(Jumpcut)* He's my boyfriend, but I'm going to change him. Because he got too much Brooklyn in him.

19. EXT: DAY. IN FRONT OF THE BROOKLYN CIGAR CO.

Customers go in and out of the store, as in Scene 3.

20. INT: DAY. THE BROOKLYN CIGAR CO.

BOB, *a regular customer, has just come in and is standing at the counter with* AUGGIE. JIMMY *is working off to the side.*

AUGGIE

A pack of Luckies?

BOB

You know what? No. I'll tell you what . . . I've got one cigarette left . . . and I've decided, you know, I was going to come here, I'm going to quit. But I wanted to smoke this with you. So I thought, "last cigarette," smoke it with Auggie. . . .

AUGGIE

You're kidding. I'm touched.

BOB

Hey Jimmy, will you take a picture of me and Auggie with my last cigarette? *(Hands JIMMY a camera)* You just push this. *(To AUGGIE)* This is it, man.

AUGGIE

All right, where do you want me to stand?

BOB

I don't know. You want to come over here?

AUGGIE

Bob, you know . . .

BOB

The last cigarette. With Auggie.

AUGGIE

I'm touched that you would want to smoke your last cigarette with me.

BOB

Hey, man, twelve years I've been coming in here . . . Luckies.

Dissolve. BOB *and* AUGGIE *pose for the camera.*

> BOB

Wait, Jimmy. Your finger's in front there. All right. Thanks.

JIMMY *takes the photo.*

> AUGGIE

You got it, Jimmy.

BOB *and* AUGGIE *sit down.*

> BOB

So that's it. One more cigarette. *(Dissolve)* I remember my first cigarette, man. These friends of mine, they stole cigarettes from this store, Bueler's Pharmacy. I still remember. It's in like a suburb of Akron, Ohio, where I grew up. So we walked home along the railroad tracks . . . opened the pack . . . I still remember . . . it was like a pack of Newports. We smelled them first . . . you know that menthol . . . smelled like candy or something. Then we lit them up . . . we started inhaling . . . coughing. Couples of minutes later, we're sick, nauseous . . . dizzy. But we felt so cool. Like, real bad-ass ten-year-old kids . . . smoking. *(Dissolve)* But sex and cigarettes, you've got to admit . . . that's one thing I'm really going to miss. . . .

> AUGGIE

Sex?

> BOB

Well . . .

> AUGGIE

You're giving up sex also?

> BOB

No.

> AUGGIE

Because you can't smoke afterwards?

BOB

Maybe. You know, I've never had a girlfriend who didn't smoke. Maybe that means if I quit I'll never have sex again. *(Dissolve)* But having a cigarette after sex . . . that's like . . . a cigarette never tasted like that. You know, share a cigarette with your lover. . . .

AUGGIE

That's bliss.

BOB

That's what I'm going to miss . . . also with coffee. Coffee and cigarettes, you know? That's like "breakfast of champions."

21. EXT: DAY. IN FRONT OF THE BROOKLYN CIGAR CO.

The WAFFLE MAN *is standing outside the store.* TOMMY *approaches.*

WAFFLE MAN

Hey, my man.

TOMMY

Hey, what's happening? *(Knocks on the store window)* Want some coffee?

WAFFLE MAN

Don't get lint on your outfit.

TOMMY

Lint? No, I hate lint. Lint ain't no good for me.

WAFFLE MAN

Let me ask you something, man.

TOMMY

What do you want to ask me?

WAFFLE MAN

I've got a job interview here at 209 1/2. . . . Say man, are there any nurses living in the neighborhood?

TOMMY

Nurses? No, there's a hospital about five blocks up on the left-hand side.

WAFFLE MAN

Yeah, I know. I just came out of the hospital, man.

TOMMY

Looks like you need to go back to the hospital. *(Pointing to wound on WAFFLE MAN'S knee)* Get that redressed.

WAFFLE MAN

No, man, it just got dressed. *(Looks down at knee)* Oh, hey. . . .

TOMMY

Well, it doesn't look like it just got dressed.

WAFFLE MAN

What day is it?

TOMMY

Today? It's Wednesday. What are you looking for?

WAFFLE MAN

(To himself, thinking) Wednesday . . . *(To* TOMMY). I'm looking for 209
1/2. . . .

TOMMY

(Gesturing) This is 211. 209 is across the street. The half is right in between
. . . right in that crack.

WAFFLE MAN

No, you're wrong. This is 209. 209 ain't across the street. 208 is across the
street.

TOMMY

211. Okay, 209 is here. 211 . . . so 209 1/2 is right in between these two
buildings.

WAFFLE MAN

I don't need no information from you.

TOMMY

What are you doing here?

WAFFLE MAN

You, you don't know nothing.

TOMMY

Look, this is Brooklyn. We don't go by numbers. What are you looking for?
What business are you looking for?

WAFFLE MAN

I'm looking for four dollars and ninety-five cents. To get a Belgian waffle,
man.

TOMMY

Ahh. You're looking for four dollars and ninety-five cents.

WAFFLE MAN

(Showing a Belgian waffle menu to TOMMY) Is that a work of art, man, or
what?

TOMMY

(*Looking at menu*) That's beautiful. They don't make those anymore.
Obsolete. They don't make them anymore. You can't get that. You've got
to go home to mama to get that. (*Pause*) That looks pretty good, actually.
. . .

*Dissolve. A Belgian waffle poster appears on screen. Dissolve back to the
street. The* WAFFLE MAN *is alone, licking the menu.*

22. CARD

Words appear on screen: "The fortune cookie said: How You Look Depends
on Where You Go."

23. BROOKLYN RESIDENT INTERVIEW

Shot in video. Apartment interior.

CHEIF BEY

Brooklyn has everything. It has little rivers running through it. People
don't know it. It has waterfalls in it . . . and they don't know where it's at.
It's just fantastic. It's a big, beautiful borough. It has everything. Flat
lands, high lands, low lands, wooded lands. And even swamps.
(*Jumpcut*). When you look at the other boroughs and compare them all,
Brooklyn is larger . . . and it's the hippest of all the boroughs.

24. INT: DAY. THE BROOKLYN CIGAR CO.

AUGGIE *and* TOMMY *are alone in the store, talking. The* RAPPER *enters
with a briefcase full of watches.*

RAPPER

Check it out, check it out, I got the clocks, the watches, I don't deal in
Swatches. Seiko, Casio, Timex, Rolex . . . what do you need when you

have sex the latex. *(Plunks briefcase on counter and opens it)* How you doing, man? I got it all, baby.

                              AUGGIE
(Amused) I'll take the whole batch.

                              RAPPER
Really, you like my sales pitch? I've got the real deal, man. I've got a good deal for you today. For you, Mr. Brooklyn Cigar Company. . . .

                              TOMMY
What've you got?

                              RAPPER
I've got twenty- and twenty-five-dollar prices.

                              TOMMY
Twenty and twenty-five dollars?

                              RAPPER
I've got the African price, I've got the European price. Which one you want?

                              TOMMY
African price? European price? Show me something nice.

                              RAPPER
Well, take a look, baby. I'll get to what that means in a minute. I'm dealing with the African first. Black people first, always.

                              TOMMY
Rolex?

                              RAPPER
Rolex, baby. It's the real deal, lizard skin.

                              TOMMY
Where did you get this?

RAPPER

Don't you worry yourself about that, baby. I got the goods. Ain't nothing to worry about.

TOMMY

(Examining watch) You're going to sell me this Rolex for twenty, twenty-five, thirty, forty, fifty . . . what is it?

RAPPER

African price? Twenty-five dollars.

TOMMY

What does that mean? I'm not from Africa.

25. EXT: DAY. IN FRONT OF THE BROOKLYN CIGAR CO.

One by one, three people recite the following statistics:

MAN

There are 872,702 African Americans. . . .

TEENAGE BOY

412,906 Jewish people. . . .

YOUNG WOMAN

462,411 Hispanic people living in Brooklyn.

26. INT: DAY. THE BROOKLYN CIGAR CO.

Continues from Scene 24.

RAPPER

Name one black person hanging around this neighborhood. What are you doing here, man?

TOMMY

My name is Tommy Fanelli. That's my name.

RAPPER

(Imitating Brooklyn-Italian accent) Tommy Fanelli? Yo, Tommy Fanelli, are you from Brooklyn or something? This guy . . . please! *(Jumpcut).* Why are you hanging out in this neighborhood, man? Crown Heights, Howard Beach. We're Brooklyn, man. Brooklyn. Bed-Stuy, do or die. That's where I'm from.

TOMMY

This is my neighborhood.

RAPPER

Your neighborhood? Fanelli. How'd you get the name Fanelli?

TOMMY

I'm from Italy.

RAPPER

Italy?

TOMMY

My father's Italian, my mother's black.

RAPPER

What's that . . . mulatto? You ain't no mulatto. You're black as me, man.

AUGGIE

Hey, hey . . . come on. . . .

TOMMY

Wait. How do you know what I am?

RAPPER

I'll tell you this, black man. . . .

TOMMY

You're assuming.

RAPPER

I'll tell you this, black man. I'll tell you this, my brother, my brother Fanelli
. . . I'll tell you this. . . .

TOMMY

Calm down. Get real. Get real with me. Talk to me.

RAPPER

Let me take a seat over here. *(Just as he is about to sit down, VINNIE
enters the store)* Hold up, hold up, hold up. . . . *(The RAPPER goes for his
watches)*

AUGGIE

He doesn't want a watch. He owns the store.

RAPPER

Excuse me, sir. Timex, Rolex, Casio, Seiko, whatever you want, I've got
for you. Come on, man, I'm trying to sell you. . . . *(To TOMMY)* The
problem is, while I'm trying to sell these watches, I'm really a rapper.
That's my thing. I rap. You all like rap music? *(To AUGGIE)* You probably
don't like it.

VINNIE

(Disappearing behind the counter to fetch his guitar) You're a rapper?

RAPPER

(To TOMMY) You probably ain't into rap music either. *(To VINNIE)* I'm
trying to get some equipment, man. You want to buy a watch?

VINNIE

(Emerging from behind the counter) My heart is heavy with song. *(He
begins to play and sing a country-western tune)*

RAPPER

(Interrupting) Hold up. What's with you people? What are you, Puerto
Rican? *(To TOMMY)* You black? *(To VINNIE)* Billy Ray Cyrus. What's up
with this neighborhood, man?

VINNIE

Billy Ray who?

RAPPER

You all want to be white. That's the problem, man. Playing that . . . whatever that is . . . that acoustic . . . country. . . .

TOMMY

This guy is good.

VINNIE

Where are you from?

TOMMY

He doesn't know where he's from.

RAPPER

Bed-Stuy. I *was* from Africa. But in case you don't remember, they stole us from Africa. *(Muttering)* Black man . . . Fanelli. . . .

AUGGIE

I stole you from Africa? Can I give you back?

27. INT: DAY. THE BROOKLYN CIGAR CO.

The MAN WITH UNUSUAL GLASSES, *as before.*

MAN

I couldn't have been unhappier in the eight years I spent growing up in Brooklyn. But I say that not having realized what it would then be like being on Long Island, which was infinitely worse. And if there was probably a childhood trauma that I had . . . other than the Dodgers leaving Brooklyn, which, if you think about it, is a reason why some of us are imbued with a cynicism that we never recovered from. Obviously, you're not a Mets fan. And you can't possibly be a Yankee fan. So baseball is eliminated from your life. Because of being born in Brooklyn.

OFF-SCREEN VOICE

You cared about the Dodgers as a kid?

MAN

Very much. I don't know why. I don't like baseball. But of course maybe I

don't like baseball because the Dodgers aren't here anymore. And these days if you said the Dodgers, no one knows what you're talking about. They think you're talking about Los Angeles—and I don't mean the Los Angeles Dodgers. But Long Island . . . was terrible, absolutely terrible. I mean, at least in Brooklyn you could walk around.

28. INT: DAY. THE BROOKLYN CIGAR CO.

Continues from Scene 26.

                    RAPPER
I'm from Brooklyn, man.

                    VINNIE
You want to hear a Brooklyn song?

                    RAPPER
You got some Brooklyn tunes?

                    VINNIE
Yeah.

VINNIE *starts playing a Spanish song.* TOMMY *and the* RAPPER *stand up and dance. Cut to a video montage of Brooklyn streets and inhabitants as the song continues. Then, back to the store:*

RAPPER

Old man, old man, let me hold it for a second.

VINNIE

Oh, you play?

RAPPER

Yeah, man, I know something.

VINNIE

(To AUGGIE) Sells watches, plays.

RAPPER

(Taking guitar from VINNIE) Told you. *(Begins to play and sing)* Yeah, ha, check it, check it, check it out. Come buy my watches, I got the clock, I got the time, I got the rhyme. Black man, black man, you're out of your mind. Sitting over here on your black behind. Sitting in the chair, white man over there, stares at me without a care. I know you don't care. . . . Oh . . . *(waving hands)* . . . whatever. . . .

29. BROOKLYN RESIDENT INTERVIEW

Continues from Scene 23.

CHEIF BEY

My favorite thing about Brooklyn is that every nationality in the world is in Brooklyn. *(Jumpcut).* The least favorite thing? That all these nationalities have not been able to get along.

30. EXT: DAY. IN FRONT OF THE BROOKLYN CIGAR CO.

One by one, two people recite the following statistics:

                    MAN
There are 3,268,121 potholes in Brooklyn.

                YOUNG WOMAN
There were 32,979 cars stolen in Brooklyn last year. And one of them was mine.

31. INT: DAY. THE BROOKLYN CIGAR CO.

Continues from Scene 20.

                    BOB
You know, I think a lot of people start smoking because it's glamorized
. . . like Hollywood. In the movies. You know, you see Marlon Brando,
you see James Dean smoking a cigarette. Marlene Dietrich. . . .

                  AUGGIE
That's how I started smoking.

                    BOB
Yeah?

                  AUGGIE
I started smoking because when I was a boy, a teenager, I saw this great
movie called *A Walk in the Sun.* You ever see it?

                    BOB
No.

                  AUGGIE
Richard Conte . . . umm . . . who was the other guy, I forget his name. . . .
Anyway, they're on the campaign in Europe. It's World War Two, and

they're in the army. Richard Conte is a machine gunner, and he has his assistant, who carries the bullets and all that . . . or he carries the machine gun. And as they're walking down the road on to the next battle, Richard Conte will be philosophizing about life, and he'd go, "Butt." He never had any cigarettes. And his partner would always go, "Ahhh." And somehow, the way Richard Conte would be walking in the sun carrying his machine gun . . . and would go, "Butt," it made me want to smoke. I used to do it to my friends in the pool room.

BOB

Yeah?

AUGGIE

I'd go "Butt," and they'd go . . . "Get the fuck out of here."

Dissolve.

BOB

Speaking of movies . . . I was thinking, too—this is unrelated—but I was thinking . . . I was watching TV the other night, in Japan . . . There was some movie on, and why is it in every movie there's a shootout, and when they run out of bullets—click, click—they fling the gun away? Like it's a disposable cigarette lighter or something. What's up with that? Guns cost a lot of money. Can't you reload it? You know what I'm saying? They always—click—throw the gun out.

AUGGIE

That's a good point.

BOB

And another thing in movies I think is real weird . . . like war movies . . . Nazis in movies. . . . Why do they always smoke like in some weird way . . . like this? *(Sticks cigarette between third and fourth fingers and pretends to burn AUGGIE. Then sticks cigarette between thumb and index finger and squints)* Yah, vee haf vays of making you talk, Auggie. Is it like the threat of a burn . . . torture? Or it's like this. Yah, vee know who you are, vee haf seen vhat you've done. *(Dissolve).* The fucked-up thing though is like, you go to Hollywood now—they got us hooked on cigarettes, we see all this image of glamour—you go out there now, you can't smoke anywhere. It's like . . . you smoke, you light up after a meal in a restaurant, they come over *(imitating a prissy voice)* "I'm sorry, sir, smoking's prohibited by law in restaurants." What's up with that? They get you started, you know?

32. CLIP FROM A *WALK IN THE SUN*

FIRST SOLDIER (RICHARD CONTE)
(Snapping his fingers) A butt.

SECOND SOLDIER (GEORGE TYNE)
What happened to the one I just gave you?

FIRST SOLDIER
I sent it home. They're cutting down on the butts at home. *(Snaps fingers)*
A butt. *(FIRST SOLDIER hands him a cigarette)* A match. *(He lights up)*
Thanks. It pays to have friends.

33. INT: DAY. THE BROOKLYN CIGAR CO.

The MAN WITH UNUSUAL GLASSES, *as before.*

MAN
Yes, I'm smoking cigarettes . . . and many of my friends have died of it.
On the other hand, while I am smoking cigarettes, I am not downing a
bottle of scotch . . . in fifteen minutes. So, looked at from that point of
view, it's a health tool. *(Jumpcut)* I can't remember the first time I had a
cigarette. I can remember the first time I had a thing . . . well, you would
know, because you're from Brooklyn . . . called a punk. Do you
remember a punk? A punk was this long green piece of wood. It was a
slim piece of wood *(holding out his hands)* this big. Dyed green, with
God-knows-what caked on it about three inches down, all the way to
the end. And you lit it . . . and pretended to smoke it. Of course, you
couldn't inhale it, because it's solid wood . . . and you'd walk around
with it. And it was called a punk. Am I right? That I can remember.
When that turned into an actual Marlboro . . . I honestly don't recall. It,
along with most of my childhood memories, are not available to me. My
childhood was so unpleasant, that I absolutely don't remember
anything before . . . I think . . . age thirty-one.

34. CARD

Words appear on screen: "Patent Pending."

35. EXT: DAY. IN FRONT OF THE BROOKLYN CIGAR CO.

TOMMY *is sitting on the newspaper rack, reading the morning paper. JIMMY is sweeping off to the side. PETE rounds the corner, carrying a brief-case. He walks past TOMMY and then stops, turns around, and points at him in recognition.*

> PETE

Tommy.

> TOMMY

(Shrugs) Yeah.

> PETE

Pete.

> TOMMY

(Growing excited) Pete? Peter? Peter Maloney!

> PETE

Peter Maloney.

> TOMMY

Oh my God! Oh shit!

> PETE

Tommy. Tommy . . . *(Snapping his fingers, trying to remember TOMMY'S last name)*

> TOMMY

(Encouraging him) Come on. . . .

> PETE

Feccinimini . . . Fellini. . . .

TOMMY

Fanelli.

PETE

Fanelli! Tommy Fanelli.

TOMMY

Peter Maloney, Midwood High. . . .

PETE

Right. . . .

TOMMY

Double A plus . . . in algebra. You're the guy who wiped out the curve.
How've you been, man?

PETE

How have you been?

TOMMY

I'm good, I'm good.

PETE

I went to Harvard. Got my B.A. at Harvard. Went to Yale. Ph.D.
Interdisciplinary studies . . . philosophy and biology. *(Pause)* So what
have you been *(looking around)* . . . Is this your place?

TOMMY

(Shrugs) Yeah . . . yeah . . . this is my place. Sort of. . . .

PETE

Still in the neighborhood.

TOMMY

Yeah, I love the neighborhood.

PETE

Hey, Tommy. Mind if I sit down?

TOMMY

(Slapping the seat next to him) Sit down.

PETE

Thanks, that's great. *(He doesn't sit)*

TOMMY

Chat with me for a while.

PETE

Yeah, I will. So, uhh . . . I went to Harvard. Got my B.A. Then I went to Yale. Got my Ph.D. Interdisciplinary studies. Philosophy and biology.

TOMMY

Wow. I always knew. . . .

PETE

(Studying TOMMY) You were always wearing that hat. *(Points to JIMMY)* Who's this?

TOMMY

That's Jimmy.

PETE

Hi, Jimmy.

JIMMY

Hi.

PETE

How are you?

JIMMY

Hi. Good. Thank you, good.

PETE

(To JIMMY, gesturing to TOMMY) Has he always worn that hat?

JIMMY

(Long pause) I don't wear hats.

PETE

(To TOMMY) Can I sit down?

TOMMY

(Warmly) Yeah, sit down. *(Slaps the seat next to him. PETE doesn't sit down)*

PETE

So, you want to know what I've been doing?

TOMMY

Yeah, what have you been doing all these years?

PETE

(Finally sits. Whispers into TOMMY's ear) I can't talk about it.

36. INT: DAY. THE BROOKLYN CIGAR CO.

The MAN WITH UNUSUAL GLASSES, *as before.*

MAN

My glasses represent probably the future of glasses . . . for a certain segment of the population. I've approached . . . I went to the patent office first . . . about my glasses. And that was because. . . . Let me explain what the glasses are. *(He pokes his finger through the empty frame)* The glasses only have lenses on top.

37. EXT: DAY. IN FRONT OF THE BROOKLYN CIGAR CO.

Continues from Scene 35.

PETE

Have you ever heard of the Bosco Foundation?

TOMMY

Yeah. Bosco . . . Bosco . . . *(Laughs)* That's the chocolate milk we used to drink when we were kids, right. That's good. That's a good one.

PETE

Giuseppe Bosco was a Milanese industrialist. You never heard of him? You're half Italian, right?

TOMMY

Yeah. . . .

PETE

I remember that. . . . Half Italian . . . and half . . .

TOMMY

On my father's side.

PETE

So you never heard of Giuseppe Bosco?

TOMMY

I'm out of touch with the old country, if you know what I mean.

PETE

Well, he invented . . .

TOMMY

(To JIMMY) Jimmy, why don't you sit down for a minute? (JIMMY *sits down*)

PETE

He invented the electronic bible. Are you familiar with the electronic bible?

TOMMY

Yeah, the electronic bible. I've heard of that . . . I've heard of that. That's the one where you wake up in the morning and you press the little button and the bible verse appears to you . . . lights up . . . flashes. . . .

38. INT: DAY. THE BROOKLYN CIGAR CO.

The MAN WITH UNUSUAL GLASSES, *as before.*

MAN

I went to a space shuttle launch, and as the shuttle was taking off, I could put binoculars straight through my frames . . . because there are no lenses there. So the space scientists were all huddled around me, "How can I get a pair of glasses like that, how can I get a pair of glasses like that?" Because they were all standing there with those tacky little strings around their necks, with glasses hanging, or they had them on their bald heads. Or, I'll be in a restaurant, and when I go to read the menu . . . I flip the lenses up. And people come over and say, "How can I get a pair of glasses that do that?" So I saw what my future was, that perhaps my future lay in eyeglass-frame manufacturing. Or being sponsored by a frame manufacturer. . . . And I was going to call it "Lou's Views."

39. EXT: DAY. IN FRONT OF THE BROOKLYN CIGAR CO.

Continues from Scene 37.

PETE

We basically go out and survey people at random. And then we take their answers and funnel them into a philosophy . . . basically . . . that

will help them improve their lives. I've got . . . uhhh . . . do you, do you
want to do a survey? Can I ask you some questions?

TOMMY

Who, me?

PETE

Because I have a quota, and you'd really be helping me out. . . .

TOMMY

Right here?

PETE

Yeah, we can do it here.

TOMMY

Sure. Sure. I've got nothing to lose. Why not? Let's do it.

Dissolve.

PETE

Do you believe in God, Tommy?

TOMMY

Yeah, I believe in God.

PETE

(Writing down the answer) Okay. *(Pause)* Really?

TOMMY

What . . . don't you?

PETE

I think there's a God . . . and I'm not it.

Dissolve.

PETE

Do you believe there's intelligent life on other planets—or are we alone in
the universe?

There's life on other planets.

PETE

(Writing down the answer) Okay.

TOMMY

I don't know if it's intelligent or not, but otherwise, why would we keep going? We keep going.

PETE

It can be yes or no.

TOMMY

Yes.

PETE

Is there anyone you hate enough to want dead? And if somebody said they could kill that person for you and the crime wouldn't be discovered, would you let them go ahead and do it?

TOMMY

That's a hard one. I don't want anybody dead.

PETE

This is Pete, Tommy. You can tell me.

TOMMY

All right, all right. Maybe one guy. Okay?

PETE

One guy. There's always that one fucking guy, you know, that one fucking asshole.

JIMMY

One fucking guy.

PETE

One fucking guy, that's right.

Dissolve.

PETE

All right. Are you satisfied with the size and shape of your penis?

TOMMY

Hey, Peter, come on. That's a personal question, that's a personal question.

PETE

No one's going to know this is you. There's no names. . . .

TOMMY

Who's going to see this stuff?

PETE

It just gets processed into a computer. Ever see *2001*? It's like Hal. We plug it into Hal . . .

TOMMY

All right, all right.

PETE

. . . works on the chaos theory. . . .

TOMMY

(To JIMMY) Jimmy. Jimmy, get out of here. All right? Just close your ears for a minute.

PETE

Jimmy's got a basket. . . . Never mind. . . .

TOMMY

No.

PETE

No? What do you mean? No, you're not satisfied? What is it? Girth, no distance? Distance, no girth? No girth or distance?

TOMMY

Between you and me? The length is good. The width is questionable.
And it curves a little bit to the left.

PETE

You've got a curved one?

TOMMY

You know, it leans a little bit.

PETE

A leaner. (*Writing down the answer*) Okay. That counts in horseshoes.

Dissolve.

PETE

Okay. How much money would it take for you to eat a bowl of shit, Tom?

TOMMY

(*Laughs*) Ah! Let me tell you something. That I won't do. I mean,
everybody's got his price, but not me. Not me, not Tommy Fanelli.

PETE

No shit for Tommy.

TOMMY

I don't eat shit. It's against my religion.

PETE

What religion is that, Tommy?

TOMMY

The religion of sanity, Peter. You should try it some time.

PETE

I belonged. They excommunicated me.

40. BROOKLYN RESIDENT INTERVIEW

Shot in video. Prospect Park.

IAN FRAZIER

One thing that you do get here in Brooklyn, which I know now from having driven around the country and looked elsewhere for it, you get plastic bags stuck in trees. And it really drives me nuts. It's like a flag . . . of chaos. A bag in a tree. It's a symbol. And I used to see them, and they would bug me. And then one day I just realized that you could get it out of the tree. So a friend of mine and I made a long bag-snagger . . . for which we are currently applying for a patent, in fact. Because no one ever made something to take bags out of trees. And it works very well. It's a long aluminum pole, and we can actually reach now, almost, I would say, fifty-plus feet. *(Jumpcut)* It's fun, it's exercise, it's holding a big pole up and stretching. We walk a fair amount, and it definitely makes things nice . . . improves the tree. *(Shot of a plastic bag in a tree)* This is your basic bag in a tree. This can be recorded on film. We know that it existed, and when you come back, it will be only an image on film. Because I will have taken it out.

OFF-SCREEN VOICE

Is this your mission in Brooklyn?

IAN FRAZIER

Well, I don't consider it a mission. It's more like a hobby, something to do with my friends. It's fun to do, and it's very satisfying. It used to be, I would see a bag like that and just sort of shrug and think, "Well, there's that bag." And now I see a bag and I think, "You're coming out, pal."

41. CARD

Words appear on screen: "Dollars and Sense."

42. EXT: DAY. IN FRONT OF THE BROOKLYN CIGAR CO.

A young woman, dressed in a sari, is standing in front of the store.

YOUNG WOMAN

Once there was a Major League baseball team in Brooklyn. *(Pause)* But that was a long time ago.

43. NEWSREEL FOOTAGE

Clips of Jackie Robinson running the bases intercut with shots of the Ebbets Field crowd.

44. BROOKLYN RESIDENT INTERVIEW

Shot in video. Gleason's Gym, Brooklyn Heights.

ROBERT JACKSON

But boy, when they moved the Dodgers out of Brooklyn, I don't believe there ever was a worse day. Maybe when the war was declared. But other than that, I don't think that Brooklyn ever experienced a worse day than when they moved the Dodgers to California . . . and the wrecking ball hit Ebbets Field. *(Jumpcut)* There was nothing like it. The stadium . . . the ball park was like a little old country club. The fans all knew each other. The Dodger Sym-phony was a group of working guys that went out and played the trombone, the trumpet, the drums, and just generally made fools out of themselves . . . and everybody loved them. And they didn't care. *(Jumpcut)* The ballplayers all lived in Brooklyn. They weren't all from Brooklyn, but they lived on Bedford Avenue, and they used to rent apartments right around the stadium, right around Ebbets Field. Everybody knew them in the neighborhood. Hey, Duke Snider, Jackie . . . how are you? You know, whatever. It was like a family. *(Jumpcut)* Now? No more baseball in Brooklyn.

45. INT: NIGHT. THE BROOKLYN CIGAR CO.

Music. The John Lurie National Orchestra performs inside the store.

46. INT: NIGHT. THE BROOKLYN CIGAR CO.

VINNIE and AUGGIE are inside the store, talking. JIMMY silently goes about his work.

> VINNIE
>
> Hey, Auggie, it's a lot of money. I'd be crazy to turn it down.

> AUGGIE
>
> After nineteen years, you're just going to walk away? I can't believe it.

> VINNIE
>
> It's dollars and cents. This store's been losing money for years. You know that as well as I do.

> AUGGIE
>
> But you've got plenty of money, Vin. All those real estate deals out on the Island. I mean, you just write this place off on your taxes.

> VINNIE
>
> It's too late. We're already in contract.

> AUGGIE
>
> So the Brooklyn Cigar Company is going to become a health-food store?

> VINNIE
>
> Times change, Auggie. Tobacco's out, wheat germ's in. You know, it may not be such a bad thing for you either. I mean, maybe it's time you moved on, too. I don't want to see you turn into an old man sitting behind that counter.

> AUGGIE
>
> Everybody has to grow old. What difference does it make where it happens?

                                    VINNIE
No more free cigars, eh Auggie?

                                    AUGGIE
You really should think this thing through before you let it happen,
Vincent. I mean, sure, it's a dinky little nothing neighborhood store. But
everybody comes in here. I mean, not just the smokers. The kids come in,
the school kids, for their candy . . . old Mrs. McKenna comes in for the
soap opera magazines . . . Crazy Louie for his cough drops . . . Frank Diaz
for his *El Diario* . . . fat Mr. Chen for his crossword puzzles. I mean, the
whole neighborhood comes in here. It's a hangout, and it helps to keep
the neighborhood together. Go twenty blocks from here, twelve-year-old
kids are shooting each other for their sneakers. I mean, you close this
store, and it's one more nail in the coffin. You'll be helping to kill off this
neighborhood.

                                    VINNIE
Are you trying to make me feel guilty? Is that what you're doing?

                                    AUGGIE
No, I'm just giving you the facts. You can do what you want with them.

47. INT: DAY. THE BROOKLYN CIGAR CO.

VINNIE *is alone in the store, sitting on a stool in front of the counter, lost in
thought.*

                                    VINNIE
That Auggie, he's going to drive me crazy. Just when I get the deal
together, he comes in playing those fucking violins. Brooklyn . . .
Brooklyn. I'm supposed to care about Brooklyn? I don't even live in this
shithole of a town anymore.

JACKIE ROBINSON *suddenly appears in the store, dressed in his Dodgers
uniform.* VINNIE *looks up in amazement.*

                                    JACKIE
Hi, Vinnie.

VINNIE

Jackie?

JACKIE

In the flesh, sport.

VINNIE

Jackie. The greatest ballplayer of them all. I used to pray for you every night when I was a kid.

JACKIE

I was the man that changed America, Vinnie. And I did it all right here: in Brooklyn. Oh, they spat at me, cursed me, made my life a never-ending hell . . . and I wasn't allowed to fight back. It takes its toll, being a martyr. I died when I was fifty-three years old, Vinnie, even younger than you are now. But I was a hell of a ballplayer, wasn't I?

VINNIE

The best, Jackie. You were the best there was.

JACKIE

Things changed after me. And not just for black people. For white people, too. After me . . . well, white people and black people never looked at each other in the same old way anymore. And it all happened right here: in Brooklyn.

VINNIE

Yeah, and then they moved the team away. Almost broke my heart. What'd they do a dumb thing like that for?

JACKIE

Dollars and cents, Vinnie. Ebbets Field may be gone now, but what happened there lives on in the mind. That's where it counts, Vinnie. Mind over matter. There are more important things in life than baseball. *(Looking out the window)* But Brooklyn looks good. More or less the same it was the last time I saw it. And Prospect Park over there . . . still as beautiful as ever. *(Pause)* Say, Vinnie. They don't still make those Belgian waffles, do they? Oh man, what I wouldn't give to sink my teeth into a Belgian waffle. Two scoops of pistachio ice cream, some bananas on top. . . . Boy, do I miss those things.

VINNIE

Belgian waffles? Sure, they still make them. Just go down two blocks to the Cosmic Diner, Jackie, and they'll make you all the Belgian waffles you want.

JACKIE

Thanks, sport. Don't mind if I do. A day in Brooklyn just wouldn't be complete without stopping in for a Belgian waffle, would it?

JACKIE turns and walks out of the store.

48. EXT: DAY. IN FRONT OF THE BROOKLYN CIGAR CO.

A man, in traditional Arab dress, is standing in front of the store.

MAN

Every day, 7,999 Belgian waffles are eaten in the restaurants of Brooklyn.

49. BROOKLYN RESIDENT INTERVIEW

Shot in video. The front steps of a brownstone building in Park Slope.

LUC SANTE

Of course, waffles are really important in Belgium, but they don't look like Belgian waffles. They don't have whipped cream on them. This is something that started with the 1964 New York World's Fair, where they were heavily promoted in the so-called Belgian Village. One of the best things about Belgian waffles is that going across the country and stopping in diners and truck stops, you still see on the menu, "New," exclamation point, Belgian waffles, even though they've been on the menu for thirty years. *(Jumpcut)* The waffle culture in Belgium is complex. Waffles generally are made in huge batches, and then they're eaten cold. They're not a breakfast food. They're like cookies or something . . . or raisin bread . . . they're that kind of food. You eat them with coffee in the afternoon. *(Jumpcut)* The Belgian waffle as it's known here, with the great piles of strawberries and whipped cream, is something that Belgians never fail to be amazed by. *(Jumpcut)* I think Belgians kind of like Belgian waffles, but to them Belgian waffles seem distinctly American. They've got that big Hollywood overproduction to them, which Belgians, you know . . . it's kind of foreign to Belgians to overdo things quite in that way.

50. EXT: DAY. THE BROOKLYN CIGAR CO.

Various customers go in and out the front door, as in Scenes 3 and 19.

51. INT: DAY. THE BROOKLYN CIGAR CO.

Continues from Scene 31.

BOB

Cigarettes are sort of like a reminder of your mortality in a way, you know? Each puff is like a passing moment, a passing thought. You smoke, the smoke disappears, you know? It reminds you that to live is also to die, somehow. I don't know, I'm going to miss them. But anyway, last one. This is with you, Auggie.

AUGGIE

(Imitating the sound of a drumroll) Ta-da . . . boom!

BOB

(Trying to light his cigarette. The lighter refuses to work). Shit. It's out, man. You got a light?

Dissolve. BOB *lights the cigarette with a match.*

AUGGIE

Adios.

BOB

(Smoking) Adios, amigo.

                              AUGGIE

Adios, cigarettos.

                               BOB

L.S. equals M.F.T.

                              AUGGIE

Loose stomach means full toilet.

                               BOB

Or something like that. . . .

                              AUGGIE

When we were kids, that's what we used to say about Lucky Strikes.

                               BOB

(Showing AUGGIE the pack) Yeah, there it is.

                              AUGGIE

What'd I tell you?

                               BOB

(Studying the pack) I love this, too. "It's toasted."

                              AUGGIE

Oh, boy. They sure do take us for a ride, huh? How's it taste?

                               BOB

(Inhaling deeply) It tastes great.

Dissolve.

                               BOB

(Taking the last puff; blowing out the smoke. Then he leans over and drops the cigarette on the floor) There he goes. Thirty seconds over Tokyo. *(Imitates the sound of bombs falling)*

                              AUGGIE

Bombs away. *(After a moment, he turns to BOB and offers him a cigarette)* Want a smoke?

(*Laughs*) No thanks. I quit.

52. NEWSREEL FOOTAGE

The demolition of Ebbets Field.

                    ANNOUNCER'S VOICE
Ebbets Field, shrine of Flatbush, will make way for apartment houses. The
old ball park, standing for nearly half a century, comes to the end of the
trail. The stands where thousands once roared await another kind of
wrecking crew. Home plate is dug up to find a niche in the Baseball Hall
of Fame at Cooperstown. At the sad ceremony, Roy Campanella is
surrounded by old Dodger players Tommy Holmes, Ralph Branca, and
Carl Erskine. They watch stoically for the demolition of their old
playground. Now it's play ball again. But not the sort Dodger fans
cheered. This time, Ebbets Field has struck out.

53. BROOKLYN MONTAGE

Shot in video.

*Images of various streets, buildings, and signs . . . ending with a plaque
marking the site of the former Ebbets Field and a shot of the Ebbets Field
Apartments.*

54. BROOKLYN RESIDENT INTERVIEW

Continues from Scene 18.

                    SASALINA GAMBINO
Today is my birthday, and I'm eighteen now. . . .

                    OFF-SCREEN VOICE
(*Singing*) Happy birthday to you. . . .

SASALINA GAMBINO

That's so sweet. Nobody's sung it to me yet. *(Jumpcut)* Brooklyn will take care of me tonight, though. If I go around my way and tell everybody today's my birthday, they'll celebrate. You'll see fireworks, but they'll be gunshots. *(Laughs)* And people will probably hit me with cakes and eggs and powder socks. That's how they'll celebrate my birthday. I don't get no cake to eat it, I have to get it smashed in my face and beat with a powder sock for a surprise party. I'll walk in my building and somebody will beat me with a sock and hit me with an egg, probably. *(Jumpcut)* You all have a nice day.

OFF-SCREEN VOICE

You, too. Happy birthday.

SASALINA GAMBINO

Thank you.

55. CARD

Words appear on screen: "Listen to Me."

56. INT: NIGHT. VIOLET'S BEDROOM

Continues from Scene 17.

VIOLET

Oh, Agosto, you make me so horny. You make my *tripas* tremble. Aie, Agosto, you would be so wonderful . . . if only you were different. *(Exasperated)* That Auggie, that Auggie . . . he going to drive me cuckoo. First he say yes, then he say no. It's on, it's off. Maybe some other time. But Ramon, you see, he don't know some other time. He's going to play at Freddy's on the sixteenth. And now Agosto say he too busy on the sixteenth. What gives around here, huh? Is somebody deaf or something? I talk myself blue in the face, and still it don't do no good.

57. INT: DAY. THE BROOKLYN CIGAR CO.

AUGGIE *is alone in the store.* DOT *bursts in.*

> DOT

Lock this door. I want you to lock this door.

> AUGGIE

What's with you, Dot?

> DOT

I don't want to talk to you. I don't want to say anything to you. If he comes to the door, don't let him in.

> AUGGIE

Vinnie?

> DOT

Yeah. *(Moving toward cash register)* Where's the money? I know he keeps money around here. Where's the money?

> AUGGIE

I'm just counting up . . .

> DOT

I know he's got like a secret stash around here someplace . . . besides what's in here, right?

> AUGGIE

No. . . .

> DOT

(Opening cash register and reaching in for money) But I'm taking this, too.

> AUGGIE

Dot, what's the matter with you? It's only today's receipts. What are you doing?

> DOT

I'm taking the money. I told you before . . . I'm going to Las Vegas. By myself. I asked him to go, and he doesn't want to go. So I'm going to go to Las Vegas, and not only am I going there for a visit, but I'm going to go there . . . and I might just fucking live there. You know what I mean?

AUGGIE

What happened?

DOT

What happened! I told you what happened. He's a fucking bore. I'm going to do something exciting. I'm going to go to Las Vegas, and I'm going to wait to see Wayne Newton. And then, when I see Wayne Newton, I'm going to chase him down the street . . . and I'm going to mount him like Trigger! *(Jumpcut)* I want out, and I want to go have fun. And I'm going to. I'm going to, and don't try to talk me out of it. Because the last time I tried to talk to you, you didn't have nothing to say to me. I ain't got nothing to say to you. And I'm not going to have nothing to say to him. And you're going to tell him that for me. *(Jumpcut)* I gave him the chance to go with me, and he says no. I'm not giving him a second chance.

AUGGIE

You're not running out on him, are you? I mean, you're not packed and everything, are you?

DOT

No, I don't have anything but what I'm wearing. I don't need anything, because they have stores in Las Vegas . . . for large and lovely women. *(Jumpcut. DOT and AUGGIE are standing by the counter, face to face)* Nothing about your life is boring, right? You're just terribly excited about everything that you do? You're terribly excited about everything. Everything's like A-okay, okey-doke, right by you, right?

AUGGIE

I'm in a good place, yeah.

DOT

I don't think you're in a good place. I've known you for a long time, and I don't think you're in a good place. And I say that as your friend. I think you could be in a better place.

AUGGIE

Like where?

DOT

I don't know, I think you could be in a better place. Like, I think you could be in a better place, like Las Vegas is a better place. *(Pause)* Would you want to go with me?

AUGGIE

What?

DOT

I mean, I have money and everything.

AUGGIE

Dot, Jesus Christ. Dot . . .

Jumpcut.

DOT

I think you deserve to be loved . . . very fucking well. I really do think that about you. And I know you don't have that. And I could do that. I . . . could . . . I could do that. *(Taking a drag from AUGGIE'S cigarette)* Give me some of this. I could love you very well.

AUGGIE

Jesus, Dot.

Jumpcut.

DOT

Would you go to Las Vegas with me?

AUGGIE

Jesus, Dot.

DOT

(Pulling AUGGIE toward her) Would you go to Las Vegas with me? *(They kiss)* Will you come to Las Vegas with me?

AUGGIE

Dot, Jesus, Vinnie's my friend, Dot.

DOT

Everybody's got friends. You've got enough friends.

AUGGIE

(Pulling away) Dot, this ain't right, Dot. Dot, no. No, no, Dot, this ain't right. This ain't right. Listen, I really care about you. I really care about you, but this ain't right. It ain't right, it ain't right . . . this ain't right.

DOT

Listen. Listen, nothing's right.

AUGGIE

No . . . no . . . no . . . no. . . .

DOT

Nothing in the whole fucking world is ever right, you know? Things that are wrong . . . are good!

AUGGIE

Yeah, it could be good, that's right . . . that's right. . . .

DOT

It could be good. Do you know what I mean? It could be good. I've always wanted to kiss you.

AUGGIE

This is wrong . . . it's wrong. . . .

DOT

I have always wanted to kiss you. Just let me kiss you.

AUGGIE

Well, I can't say that I haven't wanted to kiss you, either. I can't say *(DOT tries to kiss him again)* No . . . no . . . no . . . no. *(AUGGIE breaks away)* Dot, I want you to stop it. I want you to stop it.

DOT

Okay, fuck you. I'm going! *(She walks off in a huff to the door)* Bye! *(She leaves)*

AUGGIE

(Pacing) Fuck me. Fuck. *(The door opens and VINNIE enters)* How're you doing? What's up?

VINNIE

What's going on?

AUGGIE

Did you see Dot go out? She was just here.

VINNIE

What's going on? She didn't talk to me.

AUGGIE

What's wrong? She seemed very upset. *(VINNIE leaves the store. AUGGIE continues to pace, wiping his mouth with a handkerchief. Outside, a muffled argument between DOT and VINNIE begins)* Oh man, oh man.

DOT *(off)*

Because I did not want you to come in! Do you understand that? Do you speak English?

VINNIE *and* DOT *enter the store together.*

VINNIE

You're not going anywhere.

DOT

Why?

VINNIE

What do you mean, why? What are you talking about?

DOT

I'm going to Las Vegas.

VINNIE

For what?

DOT

For what? To be . . . in show business. To have excitement. To do things besides watch you sit on the couch . . . and watch fucking TV.

VINNIE

Be in show business? You're going to be in show business?

DOT

Well, *around* show business!

VINNIE

You're not going to Vegas, you're not going anywhere.

DOT

You don't have shit to say about what I do anymore.

VINNIE

Oh no?

DOT

No.

VINNIE

Since when?

DOT

Since I told you that you don't have shit to say about what I do anymore. Which is right now! *Bing!*

Jumpcut.

DOT

(To AUGGIE) So tell him that I'm not talking to him. *(To VINNIE)* I'm not talking to you. *(To AUGGIE)* Would you please tell him I'm not talking to him? *(To VINNIE)* Because I'm not talking to you!

VINNIE

What's the matter? What's going on?

DOT

(To AUGGIE) I'm not talking to him. Tell him that I'm not going to talk to him!

AUGGIE

You want me to tell him?

DOT

What? Five times you want me to tell you?

VINNIE

What did I do?

DOT

(To VINNIE) I'm not talking to you, Vinnie!

VINNIE

Who are you talking to?

DOT

(Pointing to AUGGIE) I'm talking to him. He's my friend, too. He's not just your friend. He's my friend, too. I came here to talk to him. *(To AUGGIE)* I want you to tell him what I told you to tell him! Tell him that I'm not talking to him! Can you do that? Jesus!

AUGGIE

(To VINNIE) She's not talking to you.

VINNIE

(To DOT) Why not?

DOT

(To AUGGIE) Thank you!

VINNIE

Why not?

DOT

I'm not going to *answer!* I'm not going to *say* why not! *(To AUGGIE)* Tell him that I'm not talking to him because he does not know how to communicate. Could you tell him that? I'm not talking to him. And why not is because he does not know how to communicate. And you can't talk to people that don't know how to communicate. And I'm not going to talk to someone who doesn't know how to communicate! *(Jumpcut)* Communicating. Do you know what that means?

VINNIE

Yeah. What's the matter?

                              DOT

What does it mean? Tell me what it means. Define it!

                             VINNIE

Talking to each other.

                              DOT

Talking. But what comes after talking? Do you have any fucking idea
what comes after talking? It starts with an "L," I'll give you a clue. It starts
with an "L." It has three syllables. You know what it is?

                             VINNIE

Yeah.

                              DOT

What is it?

                             VINNIE

Listening.

                              DOT

Yes! Thank you. You win the big fucking jackpot.

                             VINNIE

All right, all right . . . I'm listening.

                              DOT

No, you don't know how to listen.

Jumpcut.

                             VINNIE

I'm listening!

                              DOT

Well, I told you what the problem is. Why are you asking me again? I
told you what the problem is! So don't ask me what the problem is!
Because I told you the problem. It's that you don't listen!

Jumpcut.

                    VINNIE

I'm listening!

                    DOT

You're not listening!

                    VINNIE

What's the problem?

                    DOT

The problem is that you never, ever, listen.

                    VINNIE

I'm listening now.

                    DOT

You don't listen.

                    VINNIE

What? What? What? What? What's the problem?

                    DOT

The problem is that you don't listen.

                    VINNIE

I'm listening!

                    DOT

The problem is that you don't listen.

                    VINNIE

Tell me!

                    DOT

You don't listen to me!

                    VINNIE

(Turns to AUGGIE in despair) What am I doing?

                    AUGGIE

You're listening.

VINNIE

(To DOT*)* I'm listening.

DOT *sighs deeply.*

58. INT: NIGHT. VIOLET'S BEDROOM

Continues from Scene 56.

VIOLET *is changing her dress, singing "Fever" to herself in the mirror. As she sings, we hear her thoughts.*

VIOLET (VOICE-OVER)

Ah, Agosto . . . You did me real good last night, baby. You always so full of surprises. And Ramon, he was so proud of you. You danced like Gene fucking Kelly . . . Las Vegas? What makes you think I want to go there? We got all the show business we need right here in Brooklyn!

59. CARD

Words appear on screen: "Once More With Feeling."

60. INT: DAY. THE BROOKLYN CIGAR CO.

AUGGIE *is behind the counter.* TOMMY, DENNIS, *and* JERRY *are hanging out in their usual spots.*

TOMMY

(To JERRY *and* DENNIS*)* I'm not talking about the game. The point is . . . I'm just saying . . . personally . . . *(The* RAPPER *enters, wearing a white suit)* The way I feel about it . . . Forget it, Dennis. Forget it.

RAPPER

(Approaching the counter. To AUGGIE, *in a heavy Spanish accent)* Are you the chief?

Yeah.

RAPPER

I got something for you.

AUGGIE

What?

RAPPER

Cuban cigars.

AUGGIE

Yeah?

RAPPER

I got some connections. I could do that . . . and you could be okay, man.

AUGGIE

What kind of cigars?

TOMMY

(Laughing in recognition) You almost had me. (To AUGGIE) He almost had me!

RAPPER

What are you talking about?

TOMMY

(To AUGGIE) Come on, Auggie, don't you see it?

RAPPER

This is serious business here, man.

TOMMY

(To AUGGIE) No, you see! You hear that voice? He was in here last week with the watches!

RAPPER

What are you talking about, man? You don't know me, man. I got connections. (Begins to laugh, exposing his disguise)

                    AUGGIE
You have got to be fucking kidding me.

                    RAPPER
(Laughing) I got connections.

                    AUGGIE
(Playful) Give me a kiss.

                    RAPPER
You want a kiss, baby?

                    TOMMY
Oh man, another scam. Always on the scam, huh?

                    AUGGIE
Were you serious about the cigars?

                    RAPPER
No.

                    TOMMY
You've got a hustle for everything.

                    AUGGIE
You like it here? Are you lonely?

                    RAPPER
(To TOMMY, showing off his suit) You like this?

                    TOMMY
You look good. Nice. Who are you this week?

                    RAPPER
(Putting on Spanish accent again) Valentino.

                    TOMMY
Valentino, huh?

                    RAPPER
The lover. The Latin lover.

TOMMY

Do you sit at home and think this stuff up?

RAPPER

Actually, I'm on my way . . . I've got a three-thirty appointment. I have a
record contract that . . . *might* happen.

TOMMY

You want to buy a bridge?

RAPPER

Ha ha, very funny. No, seriously, man, I'm very musical.

TOMMY

(To AUGGIE*)* He could do it.

RAPPER

I've got a record deal . . .

AUGGIE

You've got a voice . . .

RAPPER

God bless Brooklyn. It made me who I am today.

TOMMY

Well, you really should do it.

RAPPER

Do what?

TOMMY

Can you do it?

RAPPER

Can I do what?

TOMMY

Get a record deal.

RAPPER

Yeah, I think so. Today . . . it's supposed to happen. Three-thirty.

JERRY

Good luck, man. Good luck to you.

RAPPER

Thank you, thank you. I'm glad you guys like the suit. I figured I'd try to pull one more scam on you before I go away. One more scam on the man. You understand? *(To JERRY)* Where are you from?

JERRY

Me? Well, my family's from . . .

RAPPER

My family? Why do they always do that? *(Pointing to* TOMMY*)* He's from Italy. *(To* JERRY*)* Where're you from?

JERRY

I'm proud to be from . . . .

RAPPER

French? Puerto Rican?

JERRY

I'm Puerto Rican, Latino all the way through . . .

RAPPER

What's wrong with you guys, man?

JERRY

Come on, what are you talking about?

RAPPER

(Pointing to DENNIS*)* Now you're going to tell me he's black. *(To* TOMMY*)* He's Italian. *(To* JERRY*)* You're French. *(To* DENNIS*)* And he's black. What's up, brother? How're you doing, black man?

TOMMY

(Pulling the RAPPER off to the side) You've got a great rap, a great rap, but you've got to follow this stuff up.

RAPPER

What are you talking . . . follow up? Look at the suit, baby!

TOMMY

The suit . . . I agree, clothes make the man, but you know, you've got to decide what you want to do with your life. You're going to go out here, and next week *(To AUGGIE)* . . . next week he's going to come back, he's going to be selling used cars outside . . . tires. . . .

RAPPER

Naw, next week I'm going to have a record deal.

TOMMY

You could have a record deal. But you've got to go for it.

RAPPER

(Puffing on a big cigar) You like the cigar? I took up smoking.

TOMMY

I like the cigar. You know, there are numerous possibilities, right? You never know what life's about.

RAPPER

See, that's your problem. I don't think you're really realistic, black man.

TOMMY

I'm realistic.

RAPPER

See, last time I was in here, you really pissed me off, man. Hanging around with these white people. Now, you've got Julio over here acting like he's François. Please!

TOMMY

A buddy of mine . . . we were ten years old, all right? . . . we all dared this guy to go in and rip off this chicken joint. It was owned by this old

German guy, and we thought . . . this German guy, he's a real square, he's a white guy. We lived in Harlem, right? . . . so we dared the kid to go in. The kid had balls, right? He goes in, but the guy had already locked up the night's receipts, all right? But he had a little cash in his pocket. So the guy, he goes in and hits the guy over the head with a bottle. He gets a little cash out of the guy's pocket and leaves him on the floor for dead. All right? The guy lives . . . of course . . . the kid's ten years old. He goes home, all right? His mother says, Where did you get this money? She goes into his room to wake him up the next morning, the money's on the bureau. Where did you get this money? He's not going to tell her where he got the money—okay? She finds out the guy on the corner was robbed, she puts it together. She takes the kid, drags him by his collar back into the store, all right? The guy is there, his head is bandaged, he's doing his day's business. She says, "Did my son rob you?" The guy looks at the kid. "Yeah, I think it was him. But it's okay, he's ten years old, he's young." "I don't care," she says. "Well, he's yours. What do you want to do with him? You want to send him to jail? You want him to work for you? What do you want?" So he gives the kid a job. The kid sweeps up the store . . . just like Jimmy . . . he sweeps up the store every day. All right? Then eventually he's washing dishes, then eventually he's, like, cleaning tables . . . okay? I run into this guy ten years later. I looked at him, I said, "What are you doing with yourself?" He says, "You know the chicken joint?" I said, "The chicken joint! That was when you were ten years old!" He says, "I own the place." The German guy died . . . left him the place, and the guy is making money hand over fist.

RAPPER

See, that's your problem. I'm a black man, so I've got to sell fried chicken. That's your problem. I've got to be selling chicken.

JERRY

That's not what he's saying . . .

TOMMY

That's not my point.

RAPPER

That ain't got nothing to do with my record deal.

TOMMY

I'm trying to make a point here. And the point is . . . the point is . . . out of
something really horrible, something really great can happen.

VINNIE *enters the store.*

RAPPER

(To TOMMY*)* You got some watermelon, too?

JERRY

Naw, come on, that's not the point. . . .

RAPPER

Relax, I'm joking! I got you. Thank you. Black people have got to stick
together.

VINNIE

(Stopping next to the RAPPER *and pointing to his wrist)* I've got a watch.

RAPPER

Hey, what do you think about my suit? Hey! *Te gusta?*

VINNIE

It looks good, man.

TOMMY

(To RAPPER*)* Now where's that ten dollars I gave you last week?
Remember the ten dollars? You've got a short memory. Remember the
ten dollars I gave you?

RAPPER

Yeah.

TOMMY

(Patting him) Whenever you can, give it back, all right?

RAPPER

Okay. Thanks a lot, though. *(Smiling)* I bought some fried chicken with it.

VINNIE

(From behind the counter, holding his guitar) I've got some good news, and I've got some bad news. The good news is that you're all here. The bad news is that I'm going to sing.

Everyone groans. VINNIE begins to play and sing. The others join in.

61. EXT: DAY. IN FRONT OF THE BROOKLYN CIGAR CO.

TOMMY and the WAFFLE MAN, as in Scene 21.

TOMMY

You want me to buy you a waffle?

WAFFLE MAN

That's the idea.

TOMMY

That's the idea. So, you want to come with me while I buy you a waffle?

WAFFLE MAN

Yeah.

TOMMY

Because I ain't going to give you no money.

WAFFLE MAN

I don't want no money. I want a waffle.

TOMMY

I don't give no money to panhandlers.

WAFFLE MAN

Let me tell you something. I want two waffles. I want a waffle I'm going to eat now. The other waffle I'm going to wrap and take with me. Because my wife is pregnant and uhh . . .

TOMMY

You want a waffle now . . . and a waffle to go?

WAFFLE MAN

Because . . . there's an ethic . . . a justice code of cannibalism. And I saw
my wife's sonogram. . . . Life . . . it's a beautiful thing. . . .

TOMMY

Life is really a beautiful thing. You're going to get chased out of here, you
know what I mean? You want a Belgian waffle, go to Belgium. But don't
go to the Dutch part, go to the French part. *(He walks away)*

WAFFLE MAN

(Calling after him) And if I want a Boston egg cream, should I go to
Boston?

62. INT: DAY. THE BROOKLYN CIGAR CO.

Continues from Scene 57.

DOT

I want to go to Las Vegas! I've never been to Las Vegas.

VINNIE

I'll take you to Las Vegas!

DOT

You promised you'd take me to Las Vegas. You're not going to fucking
take me to Las Vegas *now.* After you said you weren't going to take me
to Las Vegas, you're not going to turn around and take me to Las Vegas,
because I don't want to go to Las Vegas with somebody who doesn't
want to take me to Las Vegas. *(VINNIE approaches her)* Get away.

VINNIE

Calm down, will you please? Come on.

DOT ·

Get away. All right, I'm going to go to Las Vegas. And I'm going to go by
myself. And I'm going to do all the things I want to do, that I forgot I

wanted to do, that I suddenly remember that I want to do. And I'm going to do them . . . all the things that I want to do.

VINNIE

Look, I'll clear up a few things, and we'll go. In a couple of weeks, I promise. I swear.

DOT

In a couple of weeks! I want to go right now! If you're serious about taking me to Las Vegas, then you get your shit and you take me right now to Las Vegas. Right now. Right fucking now. Or I'm going by myself. I'm not waiting two more weeks. I want to go right now!

VINNIE

All right, let's go home. . . .

DOT

No, I don't want to go home. I want to go to Las Vegas. *Right now!* And I'm going with you or without you, because I already have money. So are you going with me or not? And I'm not even going to ask you that. Forget I said that. Because you already said no, and I'm not going to let you tell me no one more time.

VINNIE

We're going to Vegas. Right now. Right the fuck now. *(To AUGGIE)* We're going to Vegas, Auggie.

AUGGIE

Have a good time.

VINNIE

(To DOT) All right? Yeah, we're going to Vegas. Okay?

DOT

Now? We're not going to pack? *(She and VINNIE hug)*

VINNIE

(Going out the door with DOT) We're going to Vegas, Auggie.

DOT

See you.

AUGGIE

Adios.

AUGGIE *locks the door, then walks back to the counter with a big smile on his face. He stubs out his cigarette. Dissolve to empty store.*

63. EXT: DAY. IN FRONT OF THE BROOKLYN CIGAR CO.

AUGGIE *and* JIMMY *are standing outside on the sidewalk. A young woman (the* MESSENGER*) dressed in a skimpy outfit rounds the corner and approaches* AUGGIE.

MESSENGER

Is this the Brooklyn Cigar Company?

AUGGIE

In the flesh. What can I do you for?

MESSENGER

I'm looking for a Mr. Augustus Wren.

AUGGIE

Well, you found him, beautiful.

MESSENGER

Great. I've never been to Brooklyn before. I wasn't sure I'd find you.

AUGGIE

Well, Brooklyn's on the map. We've even got streets out here. Electricity, too.

MESSENGER

You don't say? *(Pause)* Well?

AUGGIE

Well what?

MESSENGER

I have a telegram for you.

AUGGIE

Nobody's dead, I hope.

MESSENGER

A singing telegram.

AUGGIE

This gets better and better.

MESSENGER

You ready?

AUGGIE

Whenever you are.

MESSENGER

(Singing and dancing) The deal is off, stop. Ba-ba-ba-ba-ba-ba-ba boom. Not selling the store, stop. Ba-ba-ba-ba-ba-ba-ba-boom. I'll see you next week, stop. Ba-ba-ba-ba-ba-ba-ba-boom. I'm sending you love . . . love . . . love . . . from Las Vegas! Ba-ba-ba-ba-ba-ba-ba-boom!

AUGGIE

Dynamite, sweetheart. Dynamite. I'd say that's worth at least a five-dollar tip. *(Gives her the money)*

MESSENGER

Five dollars? Thanks a lot, mister. I'll finally be able to buy that hearing aid my mother always wanted. *(She leaves)*

AUGGIE

(Calling after her) Any time you've got some more good news, you know where to find me. *(To JIMMY, reading the telegram)* The deal is off . . . not selling the store, stop . . . see you next week . . . love from Las Vegas. Ba-ba-boom, Jimmy! *(He hugs JIMMY)*

JIMMY

We don't have to leave?

AUGGIE

No, we don't have to leave, Jimmy. Keep sweeping. Sweep all of
Brooklyn, Jimmy! Brooklyn is yours.

64. CARD

*The following text scrolls up on screen: "In the end, 572 citizens emerged
from the highlands, lowlands, and swamps of Brooklyn to celebrate. They
danced until the garbage trucks arrived for the morning pickup. Auggie
and Violet's first child was conceived in the cigar store that night. They
named him Jackie. His first solid food was a Belgian waffle."*

65. EXT: DAY. THE STREET

*We see a big block party in progress. Cut to: a close-up of AUGGIE and
VIOLET dancing.*

66. CARD

Words appear on screen: "The Players."

67. ACTOR MONTAGE

One by one, with music playing, we see shots of the performers with their names printed on screen.

68. FINAL CREDIT CLIPS

As the final credits are shown, they are intercut with the following clips:

A. THE MAN WITH UNUSUAL GLASSES
Off-Screen Voice: Why are you still smoking?
Man: I'm not inhaling!

B. THE WAFFLE MAN AND JERRY
Waffle Man: Hey, man.
Jerry: I've got to go. Listen, man, do me a favor . . .
Waffle Man: Passez-vous . . .
Jerry: Clean . . . keep a distance. Watch for yourself.
Waffle Man: You got any Handi-wipes?

C. BOB AND AUGGIE
Auggie: What does it do?
Electronic Fish Gun: Stand back asshole! (AUGGIE *laughs*)
Bob: You know, in case you get stuck up or something. Just pull the fish out.

D. AUGGIE AND VIOLET
Violet: Belgian waffle? Auggie, please, okay? You think I'm going to eat that shit and mess up a body like this? (*She laughs*).

E. DOT, AUGGIE, VINNIE
Dot: (*Brandishing a pistol*) Tell him that I'm not talking to him!

Auggie: Dot! What are you doing? What are you doing? *(He tries to take the gun from her)*

Dot: Give me my fucking gun! *(She knees him in the groin)*

F. TOMMY AND JERRY

Tommy: (Lecturing Jerry) I'm sitting out here reading the paper. To most people it looks like I'm not doing a goddamn thing. Having some coffee, right? Smoking a cigar. Hanging out with Auggie. But they look at me . . . they tip their hat. Good morning, how're you doing? They look at you, what do they see? They think you're a mugger.

G. THE WAFFLE MAN AND DENNIS

Dennis: That's not food. That's sugar . . . and shit. Do you know what that causes? Diabetes.

Waffle Man: Not to me, man.

Dennis: Oh yeah?

Waffle Man: No, 'cause I've got sugar-blockers.

H. BOB AND AUGGIE

Bob: I had a friend, man, he loved cigarettes so much, he used to set his alarm clock for the middle of the night. Like, he'd go to sleep . . . he'd set it for four hours later. Wake up. Have a cigarette.

I. PETE AND TOMMY

Pete: Do you look at your bowel movements before you flush the toilet?

Tommy: Oh, come on, Peter!

Pete: Just humor me. Do you look? Come on . . . is it, whoa! . . . foot-long floater. You don't even want to say good-bye to it. You give it a name.

J. RAPPER, AUGGIE, AND OTB MEN

Rapper: I talk on the phone a lot *(imitating Italian accent)* so people can't see that I'm black. But I really believe that I'm Sicilian.

Jerry: That's good, very good . . . I totally got it.

Rapper: You believe me. You believe me. I can't get my shoulders out of my friggin' ears here!

K. RAPPER, AUGGIE, AND OTB MEN

Rapper: That's the same problem we had last time. Because I'm a black man, you don't think that I can be Italian!

L. RAPPER, AUGGIE, AND OTB MEN

Auggie: If that was Sicilian, I'm Malcolm X.

M. DOT, AUGGIE, VINNIE

Dot: (Trying to pull down shade) Sorry, we're closed.

Auggie: Hey, Dot, you can't do that.

Dot: (The shade flies up, showing Vinnie at the door) Fuck!

Auggie: Dot, Dot . . . what are you doing?

Dot: Get this fucking thing closed. You're not going to talk to him.

N. VIOLET AND AUGGIE

Violet: (Removing her jacket and dropping it on the floor) To be or not to be, that is the question.

Auggie: (Gesturing) Jimmy, lock the door.

O. RUPAUL AND DANCERS

RuPaul: All right, Brooklyn, I'm going to teach you a new dance. It's called the Brooklyn Cha-cha. It's real simple. Okay? It goes like this. Okay? Step, step, cross, open, back, back, cha-cha-cha. One, two, front, step, cross, open, front, cha-cha-cha. One, two, step, step, huh, huh. Cross, open, one, two, three. *(Laughs)*

First Actor: Butt me.

Second Actor: Last pack.

First Actor: (As hands reach for the pack) Get your filthy hands off us.

PAUL AUSTER's novels include *The New York Trilogy* (*City of Glass, Ghosts, The Locked Room*), *In the Country of Last Things, Moon Palace, The Music of Chance, Leviathan,* and *Mr. Vertigo.* He is also the author of a memoir, *The Invention of Solitude,* and a collection of essays, *The Art of Hunger.* He lives in Brooklyn with his wife and two children.

WAYNE WANG was born in Hong Kong. His films include *The Joy Luck Club,* which he adapted with writer Amy Tan from her novel of the same name, *Slamdance, Dim Sum, Eat a Bowl of Tea,* and *Chan Is Missing.* He lives in San Francisco.

Smoke – photographer Lorey Sebastian. Pp. 24, 30, 37, 40, 43, 54, 70, 76, 80, 87, 88, 91, 100, 109, 113, 119, 124, 130, 133, 134, 141, 143, 144, 146, 148, 149

Smoke – photographer K.C. Bailey. Pp. 44, 45, 53

Blue In The Face – photographer K.C. Bailey. Pp. 186, 187, 192, 286

Blue In The Face – photographer Barry Weltcher. Pp. 172, 174, 179, 191, 199, 203, 221, 228, 231, 239, 248, 288